W9-BTF-648

BACKYARD

DESIGN

BACKYARD

DESIGN

MAKING THE MOST OF THE SPACE AROUND YOUR HOUSE

introduction Elvin McDonald   *text* Jean Spiro Breskend   *photography* Karen Bussolini

A Bulfinch Press Book

Little, Brown and Company   Boston • New York • Toronto • London

Copyright © 1991 by Smallwood and Stewart, Inc.

All rights reserved. No part of this book may be reproduced in any form
or by any electronic or mechanical means, including information storage and retrieval systems,
without permission in writing from the publisher, except by a reviewer
who may quote brief passages in a review.

First edition, 1991
Second printing, 1998
First paperback printing, 1998

Produced by Smallwood and Stewart, Inc., New York City
Design: Dirk Kaufman
Editor: Lucy O'Brien

Library of Congress Cataloging-in-Publication Data

Breskend, Jean.
    Backyard design: making the most of the space around your house/
introduction by Elvin McDonald; text Jean Spiro Breskend;
photography Karen Bussolini
        p.   cm.
"A Bulfinch Press book."
ISBN 0-8212-1776-3 (hc)   0-8212-2528-6 (pb)
    1. Backyard gardens—Design.   I. Bussolini, Karen.   II. Title.
SB473.B68 1991
712'.6—dc20   90-47758

Bulfinch Press is an imprint and trademark of Little, Brown and Company (Inc.)
Published simultaneously in Canada by Little, Brown & Company (Canada) Limited

PRINTED IN SINGAPORE

9   Introduction

17   City Yards

Pool Of Tranquility
Stylish Rooftop
Urban Woodland
Perennial Color
Townhouse Transformation
Small Pleasures

49   Suburban Yards

Unity In Diversity
A Japanese Touch
Woodland Wonderland
Clearing the Way
New Harmony

87   Country Yards

Colonial Garden
Art Meets Nature
Pondside Renovation
Historic Herb Garden
Updated Tradition
Yard With a View
Courtyard Artistry
Complex Simplicity
Restoration For Today

The Practicalities 153

Planning Your Yard
Fences and Walls
Retaining Walls
Driveways
Walkways and Steps
Patios and Decks
Garden Structures
Recreation Areas
Swimming Pools
Garden Pools
Outdoor Lighting
Watering Systems
Working With a Professional

Garden Basics 201

Hardiness Zones
Lawns and Ground Covers
Trees and Shrubs

Resources 214

Credits 224

INTRODUCTION

While surveys tell us that gardening is America's favorite outdoor leisure activity, "yardening," admittedly a nonexistent word, comes closer to the truth. For every gardener who pursues the cultivation of plants in what is construed to be a garden, there are untold numbers of "yardeners," who take pride and pleasure in what they think of as nothing more or less than a yard.

"Yard" is a truly American term. "Go play in the yard" is something most children have heard, while "Go play in the garden" is unlikely, since the gardener would immediately envision trampling and damage to the plants. In the largest sense, gardens are indeed created for the pleasure of people, but in practice, they are repositories of living plants, the needs of which always come first. If we stop to think about it, we will see that the word "garden" as we have come to know it, with deep roots in the traditions of England, Europe, and Japan, implies regimentation, while "yard" says, "At ease." Indeed, yards are for people, and the plants therein are organized and deployed with very human needs in mind: There is a lawn to be played upon, trees that give cooling shade in summer, and shrubbery borders strategically placed for privacy or as windbreaks.

Despite the fact that "yard" meaning an enclosure has roots in ancient Anglo-Saxon and European languages, "yard" as it is used in this book represents something of a declaration of independence from old-country notions of landscaping and plant cultivation. From earliest settlement in America there were yards, usually qualified by an adjective such as front, back, side, door, farm, or barn. (An early link between yard and garden is the New England dooryard garden, which in spirit is not that different from an English cottage garden.)

The yard as we know it probably traces to the writings of Andrew Jackson Downing, a nineteenth-century American who advocated treating the house and yard as one design concept, with the Victorian porch as transition between indoors and out. He saw neighboring front yards as being unified by uninterrupted lawn in what we may see now as an extreme symbol of democracy—something everyone had and all the same. Yet while Downing promulgated the idea of getting people outdoors, it was not until after World War II that Americans actually started living outdoors, a concept that originated in California and gradually spread across the country. Landscape architect Thomas Church, whose offices were based in San Francisco, lead the way in delineating a new way of expressing landscape architecture so that human considerations and needs came first and everything having to do with hardscape (pools, patios, etc.) and landscape thus fell into place.

Church worked originally in California, but his practical approach to landscape design soon made him famous and much in demand by homeowners all over America. Perhaps more than any other single individual, he helped everyone understand that yards and gardens are distinct from each other in their basic natures, each serving the needs of its owners in fundamentally different ways. While Western ideas about garden design have tended toward axial symmetry and Eastern thought embraces the asymmetrical, Church rose above cultural traditions and addressed owner needs in terms of how the space was to be used. Outdoor spaces destined for activities that might range from a game of softball to swimming to a family barbecue could hardly be considered gardens. There is no doubt Church was a landscape architect and the outdoor spaces he designed included gardens, but they were inevitably more than landscapes and more than gardens. Some were grand and expensive, others by comparison were budget-priced and tiny, yet all shared an appealing serviceability that suggests "yard" as the most appropriate term of description.

Based on the premise that gardens are for plants and yards are for people, we see that the idea of the yard is supremely versatile. The purpose of this book is to show how to get maximum use from your outdoor space no matter how small or oddly shaped it may appear. Rest assured, if your primary need is for a pool, there is a way to achieve this end no matter the size of the plot or lay of the land; more often than not the answer will be found as much or more through ingenious design than a large amount of money. One of the most frequent needs in a very small space is to be able to entertain a relatively large number of people; conversely, in a large, open site there may be a need for more privacy. And while we might think of the yard as having to do with the larger spaces associated with suburban and country properties, this book proves that the idea applies just as well to city spaces, both on the ground and up in the air. BACKYARD DESIGN is filled with ideas that can be copied or adapted to suit your situation.

Good design, which is by nature innovative and highly personalized, is the primary force in the development of a yard that rates high on pleasure. For some this could mean plantings designed to be effective on as little upkeep as possible, while others wouldn't be happy without a yard that needs almost day-to-day care. Here, in no particular order, are some of the subjects illustrated and described in the pages that follow, along with my personal observations about each of them:

Decks and patios: These all-weather surfaces give level, sound footing for people, outdoor furniture, and container plantings. They extend indoor living space but also effactually reduce the amount of ground that requires maintenance outdoors. Wooden decks are particularly useful in unifying rough, rocky, or uneven terrain, and they can be spread out from one, two, or more sides of a house, sometimes affording more square footage than the interior space. Regardless of the construction material, pockets can be left to accommodate existing large trees, or as places to plant new trees which will provide seasonal color and pleasant rustling sounds when breezes blow.

Pools: In the context of a garden the word "pool" usually means something decorative, while in the yard it implies a place for wading, swimming, and general lolling about. There are many different kinds of pools and various types of construction, thus making it possible to have one on almost any site, regardless of the terrain or shape of the lot. In-ground pools represent a major investment and because of earthmoving equipment required for excavation, are ideally added before other yard construction or plantings are in place. Usually the pool will be integrated with a deck or patio that connects with the house.

Outdoor lighting: Low-voltage electrical systems can be used for safety as well as for dramatic lighting, and they serve to make the yard accessible and inviting when otherwise it would be foreboding at best. Lighting fixtures are designed so as to fade into the landscape by day while at night they can light steps, changes of grade, the pool, deck or patio, house number, driveway entrance, or a strategically placed clump of trees or other yardscape feature.

Walkways: These can be both serviceable and attractive. They are usually wide enough to accommodate two adults walking comfortably side by side, with a surface that gives secure footing in all kinds of weather. Exact placement can be tricky, since what looks logical in plan may not turn out to be what works best in reality. Generally speaking, the shortest distance between two points will be the preferred course for a walkway. Wide, paved walkways help ease the moving of yard maintenance equipment, such as lawn mower and wheelbarrow, while narrow foot paths, perhaps not paved but using flagstones or a deep organic mulch such as bark chips, are more suited to inviting walks into a wildflower yard.

Trees: Although your yard may come with great old trees, in most cases the good ones have to be trimmed up and the undesirables chopped away. If there are no trees, they need to be planted as soon as the hardscaping is in place. Deciduous trees are among nature's greatest gifts to the yard, for in warm-weather leaf they shade and cool while in a leafless state they permit sun to warm the house in winter. Large trees offer a place to install swings, hammocks, and treehouses; evergreens can be counted on as windbreaks and privacy screens year round.

Lawns and grass: To many of us "lawn" is almost synonymous with "yard". The picture-perfect lawn that emerged following World War II is seen now as chemically-dependent and too much of a good thing. The trend is toward smaller areas of clipped lawn that are mown tall rather than very short, in order to encourage grass plants that are inherently stronger and better able to shade out weedy inter-lopers. Since the lawn area in a yard is a place for small children to romp and play, or even for the adults to spread a picnic, potentially harmful chemicals are inappropriate. One of the most important design considerations for a yard that is to be freely enjoyed by children is to keep the lawn area free of other plant-ings. Spotting the lawn with flowerbeds, miscella-neous shrubs, and various trees drastically increases maintenance and clutters the playing field. A hall-mark of Church's designs was to lay out the lawn in sweeping curves rather than squared right angles, the theory being that sinuous lines were more appealing to the eyes and more easily navigated by the lawn mower.

Ground covers: Although lawn grass is the single most popular ground cover and the only one suitable as a playing field, many other plants can be put to this purpose in the yard, and these needn't be limited to the usual English ivy, myrtle, pachysandra, and lily-turf. A recent innovation is to think of almost any plant as a potential ground cover when it is suited to the site in terms of cultural or climatic needs and is set out so that it quickly establishes and becomes so thick that no weeds can grow in empty spaces. One possibility among many is *Sedum spectabile* 'Autumn Joy', a hardy perennial succulent that grows anew from the roots each spring, flowers in late summer, and then turns bronzy red at frost and can remain in this state until the gardener cuts it back the following spring. Ornamental grasses are another popular choice, ranging from the low, dwarf blue fescue, *Festuca ovina glauca*, to the shoulder-high miscanthus, along with hardy herbaceous perennial flowers.

This is not a book about gardens, but in the end, I think you will find that it may be a more realistic and therefore friendlier gesture toward the gardener than many volumes that claim to be all about gardening. The yard can accommodate numerous gardens, such as a plot of herbs and salad makings, a low-upkeep hedge of lilacs and other flowering shrubs that may serve to create privacy as well as seasonal and fragrant bloom, or a row of peonies—and none of this need interfere with a basketball hoop and court, a playhouse, a sandbox, or an inviting site for badminton or croquet. There can also be an outdoor shower to rinse away sand and sweat and a breezy outdoor kitchen for hibachi, portable barbecue, or built-in firepit.

Considering that most houses have yards, I find it nothing short of amazing that so little has been published on the subject. A search of the gardening books in my personal library yielded not a single index entry for the word "yard," and a search of the card catalogue at the Brooklyn Botanic Garden produced only two listings under the word "yard." I am personally glad to have this book as a reference, for here in these pages are real answers and practical solutions for real-people questions and problems. This focus on the practical differentiates this book from other volumes on both gardening and landscape design. This is most notable in the second section, devoted to the practical aspects of yard design, where you will find concrete advice about adding a fence, creating a recreation area, building a deck, redesigning an entry walk, and more, as well as information on the functional uses of plants in yard design—as windbreaks, noise buffers, and practical substitutes for the usual lawn grass.

Finally, I should like to say that the ideas of this book really do work, for at an earlier stage in my life I applied many of them to a quarter-acre suburban plot in Kansas City, Missouri, in the years when my three children were quite young. By designing the yard so as to provide play spaces for them, gardening projects for me, and a patio with barbecue where their mother and I could entertain and relax, we were able to enjoy numerous activities at any given time, thus serving individual needs as well as affording parental supervision and satisfactory doses of togetherness.

Elvin McDonald
New York City

CITY

YARDS

POOL OF

TRANQUILITY

In the past, many yards lacked provisions for relaxing and entertaining outdoors. Such was the case with the yard of this Colonial-style house located on a quarter of an acre in a tourist town on the shore. Because the property is located on a busy corner, lack of privacy was another problem to be overcome.

Landscape designer Bonnie McLean was called in to turn the backyard into a secluded space for fresh-air activities and to re-landscape both the front and back to be more compatible with each other and with the traditional architecture of the house. The backyard, which was enclosed by a picket fence, and which had served as a gravel-surfaced backyard dog-run, was turned into a private patio garden. Fortunately, one wing of the house and the garage already delineated a sheltered space, and since the grounds were unlandscaped, McLean was able to use the "hardscape" elements in her plans; for example, she worked over the existing cement-slab patio rather than jackhammering it out.

The owners wanted to use brick in the yard because of its warm color and texture. They also envisioned a water feature, which would have a tranquilizing effect on the noisy environment. Although they thought first of a wall fountain, McLean suggested a fish pool, and this became the dominant design feature of the landscaping project. To break up the rigid, rectilinear lines of the yard and to fashion a looser, more fluid effect, the brick patio, which extends from the house right up to the fish pool near the other end

of the backyard garden, was planned with a pattern of concentric arcs. (The mason cut the old pink bricks, which came from a nearby demolished mill, so the sides would fit together to create the arcs.) The variations in shading and size of the bricks give the paving added interest.

The fish pool, which is 2 feet deep and 10 feet in diameter, required no building permit, since it was built on top of the ground. Because the yard slopes toward the northern boundary, three steps lead down alongside pool from the patio to the lawn area on the other side. This side of the pool is 18 inches above ground level. This height, and the pool's 16-inch-wide rim, create a perfect spot for perching. Custom-fabricated by a boat builder, the black-finished fiberglass liner gives the water a reflective surface. Although the goldfish that inhabit the pool hibernate in the winter, an electric heating device allows them to get air when ice forms. Freshwater clams, snails, and underwater oxygenating plants keep the water clear and the algae away in this ecologically balanced environment. The splashing water successfully masks traffic noises from the street; aquatic plants and a light focused on a small fountain jet all help further soothe the senses.

Fencing and plantings do their part in providing the privacy the property needed so badly. On the north perimeter, behind the fish pool, a new stockade fence was built of standard 6-foot-by-4-foot sections of fencing lumber to screen the patio from the neighbor's yard and to give shelter from the wind. Cutting the points off the top of the fencing lumber and replacing them with a cap rail gave the fence a simple, clean appearance more in keeping with an existing stone wall on the west boundary. Roses, clematis, and

A simple wood fence, painted white and set in the shade of a great old tree, is an enduring symbol of country living. Spunky daylilies poke their bright yellow faces between pickets each summer.

honeysuckle are being trained up the fence, which was stained to match the fieldstone of the old wall. Also for screening purposes, a privet hedge was planted along the picket fence that separates the backyard garden from the front; a row of dogwood trees by the fence that separates the front yard from the street shields the property during the summer, when pedestrian traffic is greatest. Just inside this front fence is a 6-inch-deep retaining wall with a 2-foot-wide run for two Jack Russell terriers, who, according to the owners, like to chase every bike and motorcycle that pass by.

Made of veneer granite that resembles the old fieldstone wall, a new stone path leads from the street to the backyard garden room. It is edged by a colorful display of spring bulbs and perennial and annual rock-garden plants in a formal border. On the other side of

the house, next to the existing driveway, one of the owners who is an ardent gardener replanted a border to bring this part of the yard back to life.

The driveway, patio, and other areas of the yard are lit by standard PAR (parabolic aluminized reflector) floodlights under the eaves of the house. Low-voltage spotlights at ground level illuminate the garden for nighttime pleasure.

Because of the temperate climate by the shore, and because of its protective surround, the secluded, waterscaped retreat can now be enjoyed from April to November with no distractions from passersby.

Visible from the kitchen, the newly planted border by the driveway (opposite) provides an ever-changing display of colorful perennials including shasta daisies, lilies, geum, astilbe, veronica, trollius, irises, and baby's breath. An espaliered crab apple tree patterns the old stone wall.

Providing a sheltered, private space for family activities, the new garden-room (above) offers an appealing contrast of textures and materials. The brick-paved patio steps down to a stone path leading to the street and to a small lawn enclosed by an old fieldstone wall and a new wood fence. Carefree teak furniture which has weathered to a mellow silver-gray sits on a bluestone slab flanked by pink granite. A rescued bluestone step serves as the seat for a small bench by the wall.

As the focal point of the newly land-scaped backyard, the fish pool (right), with its pots of water lilies and irises and its dark, pondlike sur-face, makes the small area seem more spacious.

STYLISH

ROOFTOP

Turning a hot tar roof into an attractive terrace is a challenge that many city dwellers face when they want to barbecue, garden, and simply relax outdoors as their country cousins do. This outdoor room, which sits atop a one-hundred-year-old building in a large city, shows how well such a transformation can be accomplished.

The southwest-oriented terrace, which is about forty feet square, belongs to a photographer who uses it as a backdrop for his fashion shoots, as a place to entertain his clients, and as a hideaway for off-hours recreation.

One of the first steps in the renovation of a rooftop is to cover a surface that is both unsightly and unpleasant to walk on. Care must be taken not to damage the roof and cause leaks in the building below while also providing adequate drainage. This roof sloped toward a center drain, which had been covered up when the glass-walled photography studio was built, necessitating the construction of new drains along the perimeter of the roof structure. To make sure that everything would be done correctly, the owner sought and followed the advice of a professional roofer on how to build the understructure for the new decking, which would camouflage the tar-paper surface.

What resulted was not only practical, but good looking. To make sure that the roof membrane would not be punctured, 1-inch-

With the Manhattan skyline as part of the landscape, this rooftop terrace combines a sophisticated flair with bucolic charm. Used both for business and pleasure, it houses a glass-walled structure that serves as a photography studio. Removable squares of redwood cleverly camouflage the old tar-paper surface. Low-growing junipers, yews, and other evergreens frame the views, and they supply four-season interest.

square ceramic shingles were placed under the vertical posts that support a grid of treated 4 by 4s. The posts were cut at appropriate heights to level the decking surface, and 42-inch-square modules, made of 2 by 6s of clear heart redwood, were then placed on the grid. (Joist hangers were attached to the posts to hold the grid, spreading the load of the squares.) For trim, and to fill a 2-inch space left for the expansion and contraction of the decking, 1 by 1½-inch redwood strips were added around the perimeter. The redwood, which required no finishing, was left to weather to a natural soft gray, an appealing effect that can be achieved in just a few months' time.

The old-fashioned barbecue fireplace adds an unexpected country flavor to this sophisticated penthouse setting. Built of white-washed stucco, it echoes the stucco surface of the studio structure and blends with the parapets, railings, and planting boxes. The

cast-iron firebox and cabinets with metal doors on both sides provide good storage. Slate pavers, used for the countertop, provide a carefree, heat-proof work surface.

J. Mendoza Gardens landscaped the terrace so that the plantings would not block light to the studio and would also be able to withstand the pollution, wind, and drying conditions of a rooftop location. To break up the rigid, horizontal lines of the parapet walls, Jeff Mendoza built a series of planting boxes with reverse curves. These fit together like one continuous container around the perimeter of the terrace. Because weight is always a problem on a rooftop, the boxes, which are about twenty-two inches high by twenty inches deep, were built of lightweight galvanized sheet metal and painted white. A lightweight soil mix was added for the plants.

The trees, shrubs, vines, and perennials were chosen for their different shapes, scale, textures, colors, and seasonal interest. For

instance, boxes next to the long west wall were planted with andromeda, a low-growing juniper *wiltoni*, liriope "Silver Dragon," artemisia "Silver King," juniper *procumbens*, *bergenia cordifolia*, *clematis texensis*, Hinoki cypress (*Chamaecyparis obtusa gracilis*), and *yucca pendula*. A flowering redbud tree, *cercis canadensis* "alba," near an entrance gate, produces white blooms in the spring and a leafy shade canopy during the summer. Portable white fiberglass containers are filled with perennials and annuals to supply color accents. These are often moved from one spot to another when used as props for photography or when entertaining. The lightweight metal furniture with vinyl mesh covers is impervious to the weather and folds for winter storage or extra seating indoors.

Although the terrace make-over was simply done, it offers an informal atmosphere, stylish comfort, and easy care—ideal ingredients for living outdoors in an urban environment.

Filled with "Betty Prior" roses, lamium "White Nancy," *iris germanica*, and *coreopsis verticillata*, portable white fiberglass containers (opposite) do double duty as photography props and terrace accessories.

Along the north parapet walls (above, left), lightweight, half-round metal containers are planted with a cone-shaped juniper "Mount Batten," *cotoneaster microphylus*, and Boston ivy.

With all the amenities of a country barbecue right at hand (top and above, right), the hustle and bustle of busy city streets seem far removed. The barbecue fireplace has a tall chimney to carry off smoke and odors. Slate pavers make a practical countertop surface.

Well lighted for nighttime cooking, the stuccoed brick barbecue dominates the east side of the terrace and is put to constant use when entertaining. Immune to rust and corrosion, the metal seating pieces and table have a cool white finish. The broad umbrella supplies welcome shade for midday diners.

URBAN

WOODLAND

City dwellers with rooftop terraces are fortunate to have an effective antidote to their concrete surroundings. The owners of this terrace atop a high-rise apartment building enjoy their outdoor space both for the relaxation it affords and for the challenge of growing plants in only two feet of earth.

Indeed, the transformation of this narrow penthouse space into a woodland setting of trees, shrubs, and flowers required special planning. Given the terrace's sky-high city site, wind, dryness, pollution, weight, and drainage all had to be considered. Also, here the owners wanted the hardy plantings to at once incorporate city views and provide a sense of intimate enclosure.

Begun in 1980 as a collaborative effort between landscape architect Bob Ermerins and landscape designer and sculptor Jeff Mendoza, the project was completed by Mendoza in 1982. From a perfectly barren, tar-and-gravel environment 60 feet long by only 12 feet deep evolved a series of outdoor rooms that expand the owners' living space and give them variations in plantings in each area and for each season.

Frost-proof Italian tile now covers the wraparound terrace,

Central Park and Manhattan's west-side skyline form the spectacular backdrop of the penthouse terrace.

The 2- to 3-inch pinecones that Atlas cedars produce (right) are a spectacular bonus.

which faces south and west. Pitched toward drainage holes that already existed, the easy-care, long-wearing tile is of a warm beige color that complements the building's brick facade. The plant containers, made in squares and half-circles, form a continuous line around the perimeter. To ensure proper drainage, they are raised 2 inches off the ground, have holes in the bottoms, and sit on hidden runners. Just 24 inches high by 20 inches wide, except for the larger rounded forms, the containers are made of galvanized sheet metal, which is lightweight and produces an organic look that is an effective foil to the geometric stainless-steel parapet. An architectural bronze finish, which goes well with the beige of the tile, matches the window and door frames.

Mendoza's eye and sensitivity to design principles are evident in the extraordinary selection of plant materials. They are striking in their contrast of texture, shape, scale, color, and bloom. Because the flowers are constantly changing with the seasons, the foliage plays a significant role in the color and texture of the garden, as well as in its overall composition.

The evergreens—cedars, junipers, yews, and cypress—provide year-round interest and are the backbone of the garden. Vignettes of color come from the perennials and annuals that are interspersed among them. Deciduous trees, contributing scale and shade, include a Japanese maple, a hawthorn, and a crab apple that bursts forth with pale pink blossoms in the spring. Also planted for springtime pleasure are hundreds of bulbs, which replace the annuals in the fall. Snowdrops start the sequence of blooms in early March. They are followed by crocus, dwarf irises, alliums, grape hyacinths, daffodils, and some four hundred tulips that are grouped

The redwood trellis attached to the building's exterior (left) provides a sturdy latticework support for the twining honeysuckle. The Stephanandra's bowed branches make it an ideal underplanting.

Flourishing in their southwest exposure on the rooftop terrace, the smog-resistant blue Atlas cedars (opposite) create the feeling of enclosure without blocking views. In winter, they look handsome when dressed in snow. Underplantings of Japanese juniper spill over the simple containers in a graceful form.

by color—pale whites and pinks in one area; vibrant yellows, oranges, and reds in a second; and subtle blues, purples, and pinks in a third. After blooming, the bulbs come out, the annuals go in, and the summer cycle begins. A main focus of the terrace, the blue Atlas cedars are a strong sculptural presence outside the dining room, but are not so dense as to obstruct the view. They allow the owners to be in contact with nature and still see the cityscape beyond. Six feet tall when planted, the cedars are kept pruned to maintain their graceful form and an appropriate height.

Mendoza provides full maintenance to keep the garden at its best. This means watering from once a week in the spring to perhaps three times a week in summer, when there is less rainfall. And, of course, deadheading and staking are part of the beautification program.

As with any garden, some trial and error has been inevitable here. Three tries may be required before Mendoza and the owners are successful in finding new plantings that do well. Wind is the villain in this particular location. Although a Japanese snowball viburnum survived only two years, the Atlas cedars have thrived.

Two vine-covered trellises soften the building's facade and add height to the garden. Honeysuckle climbs the trellis outside the living room that faces south; a fall-blooming clematis has been trained up the other, which faces west.

The living room, dining room, bedroom, and kitchen all open to this peaceful retreat, so far removed mentally and physically from the bustling city fourteen floors below. With two sitting areas outside the living room, facing south, and one outside the dining room and kitchen, facing west, the owners can choose the optimum spot for relaxing and enjoying their cityscape, according to the vicissitudes of wind, sun, and shade. An iron table and chairs on the west arm of the terrace provide a pleasant place to breakfast with the birds or to watch the sun go down at dinner.

Relaxing outdoors is inviting and carefree with airy, comfortable furniture that will withstand the rigors of weather and use (left).

In between the cedars are foliage plants, shrubs, perennials, and annuals that are happy in full sun (top, left). They include a red verbena, a purple-leafed morning glory, an ornamental ruby chard, artemisia, nicotiana, and an ilex shrub.

A redwood cabinet (top, right), which stores fireplace logs, does double-duty for gardening storage and for serving at the nearby dining table.

The cottage-style garden (above), with its subtle mix of flowering and foliage plants, comes as a surprise in this high-rise location. The yellow-flowered calendulas do well in the wind. The *Rosa Glauca*, which is grown for its purple-gray leaves, and the daisy-like strawflower in the stone urn are tolerant of heat and drought.

PERENNIAL

COLOR

A simple brick terrace, a profusion of flowering plants, and a little work were all it took to transform this small, once unused yard into an open-air room that affords three seasons of pleasurable outdoor living.

The owners bought this Victorian weekend house in an old fishing village fifteen years ago. The one-sixth acre property had only a small patch of crabgrass for lawn and no garden. When the couple began relandscaping, they knew nothing about gardening. Their initial project was simply to screen the front of the house from the street with shrubs they remembered from their childhood. Then they moved on to annuals planted in a somewhat haphazard fashion next to the house.

Inevitably, the planting of the annuals led to the gradual purchase of perennials from mail-order catalogues, and as these prospered and proliferated, they established the direction the couple continued to follow. Not only did the perennials send forth new foliage and flowers every spring, but their roots generated new plants that provided new stock for transplanting. Also, besides saving the work, time, and expense of replanting the whole garden every year, the long-lived perennials provided a perpetual framework for adding a few accent annuals.

A sunny southern exposure proved ideal for successfully growing a great variety of flowers in a lively purple, blue, yellow, and white color scheme. The blooming season begins with golden yellow basket-of-gold, white bleeding heart, and blue camassia in the early spring. Deep purple clematis flowers through most of summer, and the colorful display ends with violet-blue monkshood, purple-blue asters, and yellow chrysanthemums in the late fall.

A brick terrace was a natural addition to the yard as the flower beds next to the house and by the fence developed. The husband bought five hundred bricks and laid them in a basket-weave pattern on nine inches of sand, a base that assured good drainage and protection from frost heave. As he began to run out of bricks, the front edge of what was to be a rectangular terrace happily turned into a curve, softening the straight lines of the house and the

Clematis "Jackmanii" trained against the weathered stockade fence (opposite) makes a stunning backdrop for the small garden. The spectacular deep purple blooms put on an opulent display from the end of June through August. White bleeding heart, rose mallows, asters, and tuberous begonias (right) supply still more color through the summer in this perennial border. The begonias are stored indoors during the winter and replanted in the spring.

existing deck off the living room at the back. The "walls" of this outdoor room were embellished with climbing vines and roses; purple clematis on the fence and a yellow trumpet vine on the house's exterior added brilliant accents. Soil from the terrace excavation was recycled on the north side of the house, where it was turned into a shade garden filled mostly with columbine.

The owners enjoy their secluded garden in the spring, summer, and fall, and truly look at it as an extension of their house. With a hanging light fixture and a low-wattage floodlight brightening the yard, they often eat and entertain on the terrace at night—unless the bugs chase them indoors.

When the brick terrace is too hot, the shaded deck (above) becomes the favored spot for alfresco living. It is adorned with pots of rosemary and myrtle that are being trained into standard trees. A pair of rhododendrons flank the steps leading to the brick terrace.

The trumpet vine trained against the outside of the house (above) produces lavish yellow blooms at the end of July. A variety of perennials lend stability and permanence to the garden (far left). Among the star performers are Shasta daisies, phlox, alyssum, platycodon, cranesbill geraniums, and coreopsis. Annuals such as snapdragons, verbena, and portulacas supply color toward the end of the summer. A clapboard enclosure with a louvered top (near left) screens the deck from nearby neighbors, and at the same time allows air to circulate.

TOWNHOUSE
TRANSFORMATION

Because this nineteenth-century townhouse in a big city was built to its property lines, the owners had no place to go but up when they wanted a private outdoor space to escape the rigors of an urban life.

Rooftop terraces—even if only five stories up—present a different set of problems than those that exist in planning ground-level yards. What landscape architect Donald J. Walsh encountered was a basically 45-by-15-foot tar-papered rectangle with a shed, skylight, vents, and air-conditioning units occupying about 40 percent of the space. Also, the roof structure had a downward pitch for drainage; the side walls were a series of sloped brick parapets; masonry chimneys intruded on the view; and metal chimney pipes poked up in awkward places. Other concerns were the weight load, the drying effects of sun and wind in the southern exposure, the need to unify divergent elements in a small space, the selection of plants that would survive water restrictions in periods of drought, and budget constraints. Also, because the owners were away most of the summer and planned to use the terrace primarily in the spring and fall, the plants had to be chosen accordingly. However, the terrace could look less than perfect during the winter, for it was not visible from indoors.

Walsh met these challenges with skill and imagination. To avoid any damage that demolition might cause to the roof membrane, he left the chimneys, parapets, and shed undisturbed. Instead, they were painted dark gray and cleverly camouflaged to serve as a unified backdrop. A vinylized mesh fabric, normally used for greenhouse shading, was stretched on wood frames like canvas and placed over the parapet walls, chimneys, air-conditioning units, and

With its upholstered banquette, the sitting area of the rooftop terrace (opposite) offers a comfortable spot to sun and to read. Chimney pipes become sculptural accessories in their shiny new coats of black paint. The mix of perennials and ornamental grasses minimizes weight because they require less soil depth than trees and shrubs.

Screened from neighbors by the fabric covered panels, the dining end of the terrace (above) provides a peaceful corner to relax and enjoy a cup of coffee.

The latticework overlay (right) gives architectural interest to the space and creates a harmony that the terrace needed. The lattice also doubles as a trellis for Hall's honeysuckle on the tower and a climbing rose on the shed.

the shed, which had been covered in stockade fencing. To further unify the disparate elements on the rooftop, the mesh fabric was also used to face the new banquette, planters, and a tower structure that hides a pipe. Then a 12-foot-square grid of cedar lattice was placed over all the fabric to tie in the wall areas with the new wood decking. The tower and an open lattice pediment atop the shed gave the terrace an architectural quality that it lacked. The use of fabric and lattice instead of traditional wood fencing helped keep not only the weight loads down but the budget as well.

Made from cedar because of its durability and its look when finished with stain, the decking was built on two levels to allow for the pitch of the roof. It was laid over a cushioned mat to disperse the weight load and to prevent the framework from digging into and puncturing the roof. A semi-opaque gray stain, which needs to be redone every three or four years, was used to make the new floor compatible with old decking that was kept in the pre-existing dining area. The lattice grids were stained the same gray to contrast with the darker shade of the mesh fabric. All the wall panels and the deck sections are removable to permit future roof maintenance.

Planting materials were carefully selected for their low weight and ability to tolerate drought. Since trees and shrubs would require bigger planting boxes and more soil than herbaceous perennials, ornamental grasses, and vines, such plantings were kept to a minimum. The ones that were used for reasons of scale— clumped white birch, Shore juniper, mugo pine, hinoki cypress, and San Jose holly—were strategically located. The planters, which are made of redwood, were filled with styrofoam "peanuts" instead of conventional gravel, to provide more drainage, and a lightweight soil mix. A mesh screen between the two fillers keeps the soil from draining out.

To save water and to free the owners from this maintenance chore, an automatic drip-irrigation system was installed. The main feeder was placed around the parapets with "spaghetti" hoses leading from the tubing into the planting boxes.

Both durable and easy to care for, the simple furnishings on the terrace were kept to a minimum, with the built-in banquette and planters making good use of the small space. The cushions were upholstered in a colorful awning canvas that is washable and will not fade. In the dining area, an old table was given a new look with a coat of black paint and a bright green umbrella that provides shade and privacy from high-rise buildings nearby.

The airy pediment over the shed (top) adds height and a touch of whimsy to the confined space.

Weathered Adirondack chairs (above) invite friendly conversation in the central 14-by-7-foot passageway from the sitting to the dining area.

The ornamental grasses, English ivy, cotoneaster, "Autumn Joy" sedum, and mugo pine (top, left) provide a pleasing combination of foliage colors, shapes, and textures besides helping to hide the terrace from buildings across the street.

Pots of chrysanthemums in deep rusts, reds, and pinks (above, left) supply vibrant autumn color that enhances the greens of the permanent plant materials.

The fountain grass (top, right) puts forth a dramatic display of gracefully arching plumes in the fall.

Ajuga, lamb's ear, "Autumn Joy" sedum, and variegated moor grass surround the clumped white birch tree in one of the planters (above, right).

Besides adding a sense of structure to the vinyl-mesh cover-up, the 1-by-1-foot cedar lattice grid (opposite) serves as a support for vines, such as this Virginia Creeper.

SMALL PLEASURES

That a pretty garden, a comfortable place to sit, and seclusion from passersby can all be created in limited space is shown by this small sideyard. Located in a classic New England town, the 1770 clapboard house and yard are nestled next to other eighteenth- as well as nineteenth-century houses on small lots, and everybody's property is bounded by someone else's.

Its previous occupants had paid little attention to the yard. There was no outdoor seating area except for a dilapidated rustic arbor and the yard was overwhelmed by a flower bed plunked right in the middle of the lawn. In addition, forsythia bushes that bordered the street on the south side had become straggly and no longer provided any privacy.

The present owner removed the bushes and replaced them with a 4-foot-high painted board fence that had to be built on a low retaining wall to accommodate a slight incline. Besides solving the screening problem in an attractive manner, the fence cleverly solved the common dilemma of where to put trash cans so they will not be an eyesore. Bins with lift-up doors were attached to the yard side of the fence so that trash could be dropped into cans and then collected through swing-out doors on the street side. In front of the trash bins are stepping stones planted with Mother-of-thyme, dwarf spring bulbs, and veronica "Heavenly Blue."

The removal of the old arbor and the ill-placed central flower

Privacy is assured with a solid board fence painted to complement the house. Bins built into the back of the fence hold trash cans, which are emptied through doors on the street side. A rounded top adds interest to the entrance gate, which opens to granite stepping stones and a flagstone walk to the new brick terrace.

bed opened up space for a lawn. To achieve a mellow look in keeping with the period architecture of the house, the owner chose old brick for the terrace. A flagstone walk was also laid to connect the terrace with the streetside gate.

The yard's traditional flavor was strengthened with the addition of a garden shed modeled after a smokehouse in Colonial Williamsburg. Placed in the northeast corner, the 8½-foot-by-8½-foot cedar structure was embellished with a copy of a Nantucket latch that was custom-made from mahogany, and the hip roof was topped with a handcarved Nantucket whale weather vane.

The new flower garden was placed next to the shed along the sunny east boundary line. The bed, bordered by a low hedge of boxwood the owner started from cuttings, was given a small convex curve that serves as a niche for a cast-stone garden ornament and birdbath. Chock full of a variety of perennials planted in masses by the owner, the garden blossoms in a basic pink, blue, and yellow color scheme. The sequence of blooms starts in the spring with pink tulips and violet-blue iris, continues through the summer with white baby's breath, blue veronica, pink phlox, blue platycodon, pink Cranesbill geraniums, blue salvia, and yellow yarrow. In the fall, the show ends with blue asters and yellow chrysanthemums.

Three espaliered pyracanthas that have been trained against a wooden trellis behind the garden add a decorative backdrop and help screen the yard from the neighbors. A white-flowering viburnum next to the shed and a lilac in the corner next to the street supply more fragrant blooms in the spring, besides adding height and a frame for the low-growing perennials. The outline of the garden—the bare branches of the shrubs, the espaliers, and the boxwood hedge—supplies winter interest, as do the evergreen cypress trees at the entrance gate and next to the shed.

When the owner is not sitting in her garden and enjoying her colorful, fragrant refuge, she can look out at it from a bay window in the house.

The garden shed (opposite), a replica of a smokehouse in Colonial Williamsburg, helps screen the terrace from neighbors, as do the espaliered pyracanthas, which form a living fence at the boundary line. Easy-care iron furniture is painted pale pink to blend with the soft hues of the brick terrace and the perennials. The decorative statue, birdbath, and boxwood border (above left and right) give the garden a permanent focus.

SUBURBAN

YARDS

UNITY
IN DIVERSITY

Many of the American suburbs that sprang up in the 1920s and 1930s were like shared parklands. Then, as lifestyles and families changed through the years, yards were transformed to meet individual needs. This suburban property with its 1925 Georgian-style house is a prime example of such an evolution. Moreover, in its most recent transformation the property illustrates that a great deal can be accomplished in a small yard.

By the time the present owners bought the property in the 1980s, the plot, which measures only about 150 by 250 feet, and the brick-and-clapboard house had already undergone additions and sub tractions that resulted in more minuses than pluses. An attached two-car garage had been turned into a family room, and a one-car garage had been built as a replacement. Unfortunately, the new garage, decorated with a basketball hoop and a rose-covered pipe trellis, was unusable because it was extremely small and it was necessary to make a 90-degree turn to drive into it. In the yard, remnants from the past included an old wild-cherry tree with bare earth underneath, an outdated stone barbecue, and a dilapidated picnic table. Some hedges of hemlock and rhododendron had aged gracefully, however, having grown into a welcome privacy screen along the yard's borders. And a silver beech tree had matured to lend both sculptural beauty and shade to the landscape. Finally, seeming much like afterthoughts, the house and a blacktop drive-way simply sat on the lot with no garden beds, no relationship to the grounds, and no definable space for outdoor living.

These were the conditions that greeted Peter Gisolfi, a building and landscape architect, when he was asked to landscape the property and incorporate a greenhouse extension to the house, a carport to replace the unusable garage, an open-air shower, and a gateway to an adjacent tennis-and-swim club.

Gisolfi's ingenious design not only capitalized on the existing trees and shrubs but made the postage-stamp-sized plot seem much larger and more private. Most of the usable land was on the east side of the house; Gisolfi divided this land into three distinct outdoor areas, all linked to each other and to the main house in a logical and aesthetically pleasing way.

One area comprises the new driveway and the carport, which is built so that two vehicles can drive directly into it without making any turns. The gable-end roof of the 20-by-20-foot carport repeats the architectural detailing of the house. This pediment motif, used also for the shower and the gateway to the club, is a unifying

The showy snowball viburnum (opposite) is one of many spring-flowering shrubs that enhance the rosy tones of the house's brick exterior and the other garden areas.

Replacing much of the front lawn with evergreen ground covers (left) has cut down on maintenance. Cotoneaster and juniper soften the flagstone steps and walkway. The decorative pediment above the doorway of the house inspired the architectural detailing for all the garden structures.

element in the landscape design. Gisolfi deliberately designed the carport so that nothing could be stored in it; instead, the open structure does double duty as an attractive place to serve food when the owners entertain. With its basketball hoop and trellis removed, the old one-car garage is now a workshop and storage room.

The new driveway was broadened to create a turnaround area outside the carport. The turnaround also serves as a central court-yard that connects all the outdoor areas with the house. The asphalt on the driveway was replaced with precast concrete that simulates aged brick. These pavers are laid in a basketweave pattern over 8 inches of black cinders. Good-looking and durable, they cost about half the price of real brick laid in mortar. Cobblestone edging gives the driveway a finished look.

Completing the first area is a breezeway (which includes an outdoor shower) which connects the carport to the house. Equipped with hot and cold water, the shower is used from spring until fall and adds greatly to the couple's enjoyment of their yard.

The yard's main sitting area, a sunken, secluded terrace adjacent to the carport, is made of the same "brick" that paves the driveway and is thus unified with that area. Three broad garden steps connect a new flagstone walk leading from the courtyard/turnaround to this well-shaped spot. Landscape timbers make up the risers and the brick-like pavers the treads. The old cherry tree was removed, and the earth that was bulldozed to create a feeling of privacy and envelopment for the terrace was piled up along the terrace sides to form hills for a rock garden, created to give definition and more textural interest to the perennial beds that surround the terrace.

The expanse of lawn next to the terrace is an inviting place to lounge and contemplate the garden during daylight hours. A continuous line of new, curved planting beds along three sides supplies a pleasing backdrop of ever-changing colors, textures, and shapes, in addition to contributing to a sense of containment in this open, sunny place.

Even though the yard's make-over was completed in stages over several years, the total look is one of great harmony. This is largely due to the repetition of materials, design motifs, and finishes: the brick-like concrete, the gable-end roof lines, and an opaque white stain that blends all new wood structures with the clapboard and shingle siding on the house.

Gisolfi's overall plan gives his green-thumbed clients the freedom to express themselves in the selection of trees, shrubs, and flowers. Minimal maintenance is a priority. In the south-facing front yard, ground covers of cotoneaster, juniper, and periwinkle have replaced much of the lawn, for that part of the yard serves no definite purpose other than being an attractive entrance. To further screen the property from neighbors, rhododendrons, yews, pines, and hemlock were added to supplement the evergreens that were already there. Other plant materials were chosen mostly to filter the sunlight. A variety of flowering shrubs such as azalea, lilac, redbud, laurel, viburnum, and dogwood put on a show all summer; the perennials, including lilies, bleeding hearts, ferns, irises, astilbe, and hosta, pretty much take care of themselves.

So many different areas of interest are unusual in such a small suburban space, and they beautifully reflect the owners'—and today's—easy, relaxed approach to outdoor living.

Gable ends, a columned facade, and open grid sides give the carport (opposite, above, far left) a light, airy appearance in the landscape. The breezeway and shower enclosure are to the left; to the right are the gateway to the tennis club and the entrance to the hidden terrace. Espaliered pyracantha is being trained up the side of the carport. The old silver beech tree, which shades and anchors the garden, does not leaf out until May. It is kept pruned to let light and air into the yard.

With trees and sky for a canopy, the open-air shower (opposite, above, near left) is a unique feature of the remodeled yard. Its weathered cedar interior, duckboard floor, and slat benches are impervious to the weather.

The shaded, sunken terrace (above) becomes a cool, leafy retreat for eating and entertaining during the warm summer months. Rocks, evergreens, and perennials increase the sense of enclosure and privacy. The wrought-iron furniture needs little upkeep.

Mushroom-shaped redwood downlights with verdigris copper shades (left) make handsome terrace accessories. A concrete aggregate trough provides an ideal environment for growing miniature alpine species such as the white-flowered saxifrage spilling over the side.

A JAPANESE

TOUCH

Working with this long, hilly site was quite a challenge for landscape designer Jan Johnsen, particularly since the clients wanted her not only to landscape an existing swimming pool, but to put a tennis court, pergola, gazebo, hot tub, and paddle-ball court in their narrow two-acre property. Yet, she accomplished her goals with imagination throughout the yard.

Johnsen solved many problems, both practical and aesthetic, with techniques she learned during a year she spent in a landscape-architecture office in Japan. Breaking inclines into terraced landings is one of these techniques. With few level areas in the yard, Johnsen's initial task was to minimize the feeling of a steep slope in a small site, since she knows that people don't like to go up and down hills, psychologically preferring flat land instead. Terraced landings cut down on the feeling of height. To make the site seem larger, she used vegetative screening to create a series of outdoor rooms so that the property cannot be seen all at once. Johnsen also believes that

Wide grass steps have the effect of minimizing the steep slope to the pool and tennis court below. Johnsen's aim was to ease the transitions between the different "rooms" on the property.

Low-voltage path lights concealed in the planting bed next to the flagstone walkway (top left) ensure safe footing at night.

New and pre-existing boulders form the framework for plantings and structural elements in the landscape (above left).

A dry stream of smooth, rounded stones conceals an underground pipe that drains water from the lower areas of the property (top right).

A gate offers entry to grass steps and a flagstone path for access to the pool or house (above right).

From the parking area, friends and family can go up flagstone steps to the house or between the fieldstone columns to the grass steps leading to the pool at the bottom of the hill (opposite).

blocking the view entices a person to explore—that if we can see everything at one glance, we have no desire to go further. In addition, she believes that a sense of shelter and protection are important, and therefore created corners and small spaces in which people could congregate.

One practical matter the designer had to address before considering the aesthetic aspects of the project was drainage. The ground would often become soggy, particularly in the spring. Drawing once again on her stay in Japan, Johnsen resolved this problem with a boulder-lined "dry stream." A dry stream looks like a stream but holds no visible water; instead the water is carried away by means of an underground drainage pipe. Rounded stones are placed over the pipe, giving it a natural appearance.

Since Johnsen believes that changing grades and mounding add more interest to a garden, and thinks of plants as the "frosting," soil was brought in to create mounded areas on both sides of the "streams," with the boulders serving as retainings walls.

Like the dry stream and the outdoor rooms, the steps from the house to the pool area represent another Japanese approach. Johnsen says that the Japanese are fond of illusion, which she created with these grass steps. From above only grass is visible, and not the cobblestone risers, giving the illusion of a long, lean vista and maximizing the look of the lawn. Moreover, the grass steps extend the width of the open area, following the pattern of the dry stream. By making the steps so wide, the hill appears less steep. Flagstone pavers were reset to supplement the grass steps.

The designer left nothing to chance in her selection of materials and plants, or in their placement. Providing maximum seasonal pleasure was among her primary considerations. For instance, the paddle-ball court and hot tub were located on an upper terrace so they would be easily accessible from the house for spring and fall enjoyment. Evergreens such as mugo pine, Japanese andromeda, umbrella tree, yellow thread-leaf cypress, and Manhattan euonymus were planted along the dry stream for winter interest, since this is the primary view from the house.

Because the owners use their grounds mostly in the summer, landscaping around the swimming pool was emphasized. The granite decking around the pondlike pool was extended. Besides providing a surface that would not burn bare feet, the stone enhances the naturalistic character of the landscape. An existing fieldstone wall was not high enough to shield the pool from cars in the parking area above, so railroad ties were added to the top of the wall. The hill, planted with early-, mid-, and late-blooming daylilies, supplies color all summer long. Beyond the flowers are a yew hedge and a row of Kwanzan cherry trees. From the parking area above the pool, all that can be seen are the cherry trees and yews.

An existing outbuilding located next to the pool was converted into a pool house. Aluminum sliding doors were replaced with new French doors, and Johnsen added new casement windows, outdoor lights, and benches. An ornamental trellis was built to enhance the uninteresting facade and to support a wisteria vine that blooms in late spring. The square grid motif and arched pediment added an inexpensive decorative touch.

An airy latticed pergola extends out from the side of the pool house. This addition became a significant architectural feature in the landscape. The pergola provides a shaded viewing stand for players and onlookers while obscuring the view of a lower tennis court from the house.

A fanciful gazebo with turned columns, dark-green wood floor, and cedar-shake roof was built as a "destination point" overlooking the tennis court at the far end of the property. Surrounded by white pine, spruce, and rhododendron, and with boulders serving as

steps, the secluded gazebo provides a rustic escape from the centers of more sociable activity.

In keeping with the Colonial-style house, the garden structures are all white. The picket fence surrounding the pool and the bowed cedar fence that screens the property from neighbors were given a stain which, unlike less enduring paint, needs to be redone every three to five years.

The design of this yard was a long-term project that was completed in stages over a nine-year period. Working over the long term has the advantage of letting owners and designer see how the design functions and how the plants look before moving on to another stage. The next stage is for an upper hill is to be leveled and transformed into a children's play yard.

Containers of daylilies (opposite) decorate the flagstone terrace next to the tennis court.

Because it does not absorb heat, the granite decking around the pool extends to the patio by the pool house (above). Wisteria embellishes the trellised facade, and a magnolia tree shades the eating and lounging area.

The weeping shapes of a cherry tree and a red-leaf maple (left) make appropriate landscape accents at the water's edge.

In harmony with its sylvan setting (above), plantings around the pool reinforce the effect of "cultivated wildness" that the owners like. Four pear trees next to the entry gate are pruned to grow into each other, forming a canopy-type hedge that conceals the pool from the grass walkway. A free-form shape and natural granite for the decking and steps integrate the pool with the wooded landscape.

Purple loosestrife, multicolored daylilies, and grasslike liriope (left) soften the hard edges of the retaining wall.

In its remote location (opposite), the romantically styled gazebo is an invitation to get away from it all. One of the garden's intimate outdoor rooms, it required a clearing in the woods.

WOODLAND WONDERLAND

Much of the art of gardening lies in the personal imprint of the gardener. Even two identical pieces of land will look very different once their respective owners start planning and planting and building. This Americanized English-style garden is a fine example of the impact of an individual sensibility on the design of the landscape.

It is hard to believe that when its present owners bought this woodland property twenty years ago they were not even thinking about gardening. The couple was attracted to the house because of its setting on a little over an acre and its distinctive Dutch Colonial styling, with a stone and cedar-shake exterior, curved slate roof, and a picturesque Dutch entry door. A small brook in a wooded area was also part of the appeal. All that existed in the way of plantings on the property were one Betty Prior rosebush, a couple of old peonies, and three boxwoods.

The property's metamorphosis from undistinguished grounds to a picturebook setting, replete with a greenhouse, brick terrace, woodland walk, gazebo, decorative garden furnishings, and a profusion of flowering plants, happened gradually as the years passed. The driving force behind the transformation came from the wife, who did most of the work herself. A collector at heart, she filled the garden with everything she loves. Her philosophy was to plant anything that flowered and to try anything new that intrigued

After twenty years, pachysandra has taken over one side of the front yard (opposite and below, left), greatly reducing lawn chores. The owners wish, however, that they had chosen a more interesting ground cover, such as hosta, periwinkle, or ajuga. The woodland landscape now in-cludes a greenhouse addition (below, right), which allows the owners to garden year round. The tiered garden at the end of the structure is chock-full of early spring bulbs, herbs, and a variety of lilies.

her from catalogues, local nurseries, and friends. She is particularly partial to perennials, since they can be perpetuated and shared with friends, one of the satisfactions of gardening. The neophyte gardener was digging and experimenting from the start. As she went from one project to another, she read books, took classes, and attended lectures to gather gardening information. Obviously, she learned her lessons well.

One of her first major additions to the property was a greenhouse, where plants could be propagated from seeds and cuttings. When an old tulip tree next to a sunporch blew down during a storm, it fortuitously opened up an ideal spot for this welcome addition to the house. The factory-built, curved-eave design was chosen to blend with the sloping roof and traditional lines of the house. Its climate is controlled by jalousie windows, a fan, an automatic vent that opens when the greenhouse gets too hot, and baseboard heat for winter operation. Exterior vinyl-mesh shades regulate the hot summer sun. In the winter they are removed to let the sun heat the interior. Flowering plants raised in the greenhouse include a variety of orchids, some of which were cast-offs from friends, camelias, and a cutting crop of sweet peas and carnations. The wife also tends a collection of succulents, for which she has

won prizes. During the summer most of the plants are moved outdoors, where they make colorful terrace accessories, and a table and chairs are moved into the greenhouse, where the couple can dine and view the garden.

The owners nestled their new terrace into an L formed by the house. They chose brick as the paving material because of its warm, traditional appearance. The couple had originally wanted to use old pavers, but they settled for new ones when they were advised that the new brick would probably be more reliable. The brick was laid in sand and soon developed the mellow look that they wanted.

French doors open from the family room to a bluestone gravel walkway retained with a stone wall. Taken in one direction, the walkway connects the house to the terrace. Taken in the opposite direction, it leads to a new potting and storage area screened by a lattice structure that has been painted gray to match the house shutters. Elliptical and circular beds were planned as part of the terrace design, to break up its flat expanse and impart a decorative touch in the English tradition. All the boxwoods that form the ovals were started on the site with cuttings from the original specimens on the property. They are kept clipped to maintain a low profile. Inside these frames, such annuals as easy-care begonias assure

Influenced by traditional English garden design, the brick terrace (opposite, left and right) is warm and inviting. A collection of antique furniture, selected piece by piece through the years, supplies old-world charm and comfortable seating. Candytuft edges the stone path, thyme grows between the paving steps, and wisteria climbs up the corner of the sunroom. Boxwoods, started from cuttings, provide a neat frame for a bed of begonias (above). Garden ornaments add decorative interest and a touch of whimsy throughout the yard and terrace. Fortunately, the brass rabbits (right) leave the plants alone.

colorful blooms throughout the summer. A dramatic yucca dominates the circular bed. The owner's collection of garden ornaments, all acquired piece by piece from tag sales, flea markets, antique shops, and friends, gives the terrace a distinctive personality. Low-voltage lighting scattered among the plantings casts a soft glow for nighttime use.

Low dry-set stone walls were built throughout the property to delineate paths and garden areas. Flowers, trees, shrubs, vines, and ground covers were added little by little. Surrounding the terrace and scattered around the yard, such bulbs as aconite, scilla, crocus, muscari, daffodils, and tulips supply glorious and welcome color in the spring. During the late spring and summer, perennials take over. Favorites include trollius, geranium "Johnson's Blue," Lady's Mantle, anemone "Honorine Jobert," coreopsis "Sunray," hellebores, lavender "Hidecote," sedum "Autumn Joy," primula, and Dicentra eximia "Alba." Shrubs and trees, the backbone of any garden, assure privacy at the perimeter of the property and provide accents throughout the yard. Favorite species include the fragrant snowball viburnum, witch hazel, spirea, crab apples, weeping cherry, dogwood, scintillation rhododendrons, purple beech, ornamental plum, Carolina allspice, smoke bush, magnolias, azaleas, forsythia, broom, old shrub roses, and Japanese maple. Vines, such as climbing hydrangea, clematis, wisteria, and honeysuckle supply more treats for the eye and nose, and ground covers are replacing more and more of the lawn.

As the plantings have increased and the lawn area has decreased, mowing chores on the property have been reduced from over two hours to less than an hour a week. This agreeable trend has led the couple to develop the woodsy area around the small brook into a wildflower garden. Simple wood chip paths permit a walk among such plants as trillium, Japanese iris, ferns, marsh marigolds, and turkscap lilies, which are an endangered species. (Seeds and scales of this rare lily have been passed on to friends for perpetuation.) Also hiding in the woods is a compost pile where leaves, grass, fertilizer, and soil are turned into mulch for the garden beds, a must to keep in moisture and to hold down weeds.

The owners had always wanted a gazebo, and eventually one went up at the edge of the woodland area. Built before manufactured models became so readily available, this romantic Victorian

Lending interest to the far end of the terrace, a sprightly moon goddess scampers through the greenery. The elliptical boxwood beds and central circle are pleasing plant forms that give the terrace extra eye-appeal.

structure, with a wonderful bell-shaped roof of hand-cut cedar-shakes, was designed by an architect. An important focus in the garden, the gazebo is a pleasure to look at and sit in during warm weather, and it becomes a source of visual enchantment in the winter, when it is covered with snow or decorated for Christmas.

The garden at the end of the greenhouse was the last to go in. Edged in brick and terraced with railroad ties, it contains sun-loving plants, including a row of chives along the border. With this garden in place, the owners claim they have run out of space. However, with their greenhouse plants growing in the winter, more beds are bound to appear the next spring.

The owner's collection of orchids includes this exotic specimen (opposite, top left) which was started from a cutting sixteen years ago. The wispy blooms provide a pleasing foil for the weathered cedar-shake siding. An antique wire plant stand (opposite, top right) makes a fanciful terrace accessory and a sunny spot for pots of orchids and other greenhouse plants that summer outdoors. With its rosy, daisylike flowers, the purple coneflower *Echinacea purpurea* (opposite, below) is one of the large variety of perennials that brighten the garden in mid-summer.

Lattice (left) provides a decorative screen for the storage shed that was built against the side of the house. Accessible from the gravel walk outside the family room, the simple structure is handy for potting as well as for storing pots, soil, and other garden supplies. The lift-up door (above) offers some shade, and a tag-sale dog stands guard at the entrance gate. In the ground and in containers, colorful flowering plants are everywhere.

The woodland garden (left) effectively combines ornamental trees, shrubs, perennials, vines, and ground covers for seasonal color and year-round interest. The removal of large ash and oak trees brought in more light and air, but even so no area receives more than five or six hours of direct sun a day. The European ginger surrounding the gazebo (above) is one of the many ground covers that have replaced grass throughout the yard. Others that have been tried with success are sweet woodruff, hosta, lamium, plumbago, epimedium, ferns, astilbe, and liriope. Two spring-blooming and one fall-blooming clematis adorn the latticed side panels of the gazebo. The large boxwood next to the squirrel at the edge of the woodland path (opposite, above) is one of the original shrubs. Dark-green mesh seating pieces make handsome garden accessories. Although the bright-red birdhouse (opposite, below) adds a lively accent, it has acquired no tenant.

CLEARING

THE WAY

For many years, the owners of this 3½-acre Connecticut property near Long Island Sound accepted and enjoyed their heavily treed site as it was. When their children were small, having no lawn and using pachysandra as ground cover meant minimal maintenance and more time to go to the beach. After the children grew up and the couple's interests changed, going to the beach became less appealing and staying home more so.

Thus, when the owners called on architect Frank Gravino, who had expanded their 1950s ranch-style house through the years, to design a new master suite, they decided to also build an outdoor living area including a swimming-pool facility. It hurt a bit to clear so many trees, but they were pleasantly surprised by how much they liked having an open, sunny space and grass to walk on.

The owners kept their front yard as woodsy and informal as ever, but decided on a more formal, traditional look for the back. In order to build the pool and terrace, Gravino had to blast and remove truckloads of large rocks that were part of the gently sloping terrain. A large boulder that was thus exposed served as a serendipitous sculptural accent at the far end of the pool, and a stony ledge behind the terrace became a rock garden. Closely related to each other, the house and the pool area are connected by a

Integrated design and materials are responsible for the harmony between the remodeled house and the new outdoor living space. Clad in vertical boards and horizontal beveled siding, the new master suite is painted a soft blue-gray, accented by deeper-toned and white trim. These hues and the geometry of the exterior extend to the landscape plan. The perennial border, with its mix of old-fashioned foliage and flowering plants, softens the rectilinear lines of the pool and can be enjoyed by family and friends as they relax on the terrace nearby.

4-foot-wide bluestone walkway. Bluestone steps, which are flanked by fieldstone retaining walls, lead down to the terrace just above the pool and pool itself. Fieldstone risers between the treads complement the rocky ledge and further unify the area.

Gravino's up-to-date interpretation of traditional and modern architectural elements is carried through both the house and pool structures. The horizontal and vertical siding and the grid of the windows of the house are repeated in the fence, and the classic gabled roof, updated for the house, is echoed in the pool house. Also given a contemporary flair is the latticework, which adds visual charm, as it has done through the ages.

Detailing gives the 16-square-foot pool house great style. With tapered columns and an ornamented facade, this open-air room, which faces south, provides relief from the sun and a shaded space to entertain and eat outdoors. A sink, a refrigerator, storage cabinets, and a tiled countertop are readily accessible along the back wall. At the rear are a shower and a closet for pool supplies.

Oriented in an east-west direction, the 20-by-40-foot Gunite pool, with its aqua-blue water, sparkles in its bright, sunny setting. The bluestone paving has been continued for the coping, decking, and terrace, which is up two steps. Tucked under the coping, an automatic electric pool-cover offers many pluses. With a push of a button, it unrolls to keep heat in at night and leaves out in the fall. Also, it provides an extra safeguard when the owners are away. When it rains, however, a sump pump is sometimes needed to remove water from the cover.

Handsomely styled with the same careful attention to detail that marks the rest of the project, the custom-made cedar fence that encloses the yard does much more than satisfy building codes. The verticals, horizontals, squares, and diamonds tease the eye, and the latticework, and peepholes let in cooling breezes.

Landscape designer Tom Gilmore planned the borders, beds, and edges to complement Gravino's well-defined plan. Pockets of soil in the exposed ledge behind the terrace were filled with low-growing shrubs and perennials that emphasize contrasting foliage rather than flowers. Bar Harbor creeping juniper, wooly thyme, sedum "Autumn Joy", heather, and dwarf mugo pine vary the textures, shapes, and colors. Gilmore comments that since some of the plants would not tolerate the high iron content of the rocks, he had to try several varieties to determine what would grow best.

The pastel heathers blend well with the plants in the perennial

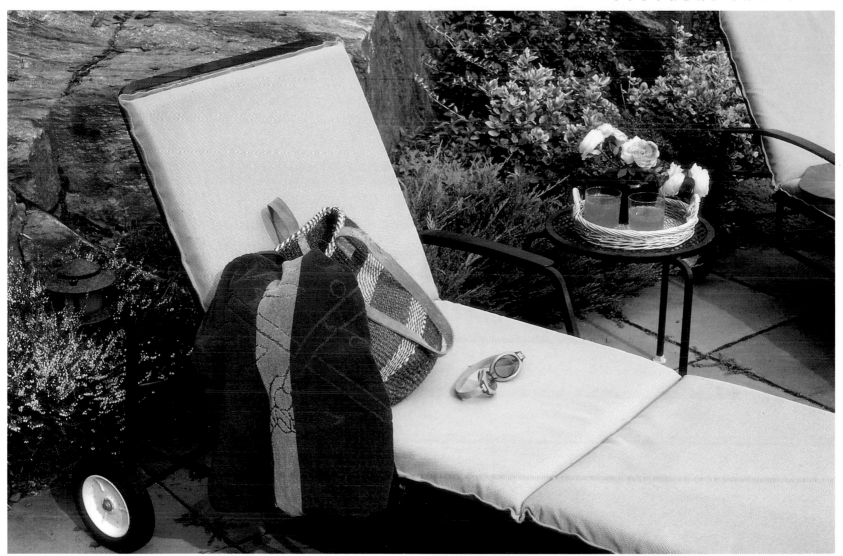

Besides adding design interest and meeting security codes, the 6-foot-high fence (opposite, top) screens the outdoor living area from neighboring houses. The crimson pigmy barberry edging the fence gives balance to the holly hedge on the other side of the pool.

A distinctive part of the fence design, the small square openings (opposite, middle) break up the wind and lead the eye outward.

The 4-foot-high fence by the house (opposite, bottom) follows the contours of the land. The latticed gate opens to the wooded part of the front yard.

The rocky ledge forms a picturesque backdrop for relaxing and sunning by the pool (above).

A pleasing part of the interplay of materials and textures, the bluestone steps to the terrace (right) are enhanced by the fieldstone risers and retaining walls.

border along the long side of the pool. The garden, the soft, magical quality of which the owner compares to a Monet painting, is 8 feet deep by 40 feet long and blooms throughout the summer in a wondrous palette of blues, pinks, purples, and whites. Included are groupings of heather, lavender, Nikko blue hydrangea, astilbe, hollyhock, mallow, and phlox. The only annual, "Prairie Gentian," added each spring, anchors the garden with its deep-blue, bell-shaped flowers that last most of the season. A 2-foot-deep hedge of Blue Princess holly rims this bed. At the far-west boundary of the pool, stands of *arborvitae nigra*, which look like sentinels at each corner, delineate the formal aspect of the yard. A back hedge of juniper hetzi and a weeping cherry complete the sense of enclosure.

Rock had to be blasted before the terrace could be built. A remaining ledge was turned into a garden for miniature alpine plants and other low-growing evergreens (above). The arborvitae and juniper at the far end of the pool help smooth the transition from the formality of the plantings to the natural landscape.

With its playful adaptation of architectural details from the past, the pool house (opposite, above) is the dramatic focus of the remodeled yard. The open circle on the gable end is aligned with the passageway to the house. The tones of the quarry-tile floor blend with those of the bluestone paving.

The pool house is well equipped for serving alfresco meals (opposite, left and right). It offers welcome shade for sunny-day lunches, while lighting makes poolside dining a joy after dark as well.

NEW

HARMONY

When old country estates are broken up and sold off as lots, with or without houses and other outbuildings, the properties often have character but lack individuality. The owners of this one acre property discovered this when they bought it as a weekend retreat. All the basics were already there. In the 1920s, when the large acreage was divided into parcels, this particular one included a carriage house and a tennis court. By the time the present owners bought it, the original horse-and-buggy structure had not only been converted into a residence, but a swimming pool, pool house, and guest house had been added. In addition, the setting itself was lovely, with statuesque trees and old stone walls embellishing the landscape.

Yet while the ambience and the amenities were irresistible, the grounds, which had no gardens, no terraces, and no sense of unity, were nondescript and needed a lot of work. The carriage house, pool, tennis court, and guest quarters all required overhauling.

The owners lived in the two-bedroom guest house while utilities were replaced in the main house and it was refurbished with new floors, windows, French doors, dark green shutters, and fresh coats of white paint. A landscape architect was called in to connect the property's diverse elements, to revitalize the grounds, and to create an outdoor area that would be an extension of the indoor space.

The siting of the house itself was unusual. Because it sat on the highest point of sloping terrain near the back perimeter of the property, everything was located in the front yard. The house's

All garden areas of the remodeled carriage house are in the front yard. The latticed fencing and perennial beds tie together the divergent elements of the landscape.

facade looked out over the pool, down to the tennis court, and beyond to the guest house. Unfortunately, all of these components lacked cohesion.

Eventually, a harmonious look was achieved with a simple plan that was both practical and aesthetically pleasing. They made use of the gentle incline to build a stone retaining wall, which created space for an expansive upper terrace accessible from the living room, dining room, front entry, and the kitchen. The retaining wall was constructed of granite, cut into rectangular shapes, mortared, and capped with flagstone in a monochromatic gray. The same flagstone was also cut into rectangles and mortared on a concrete base for the terrace. Because the exit from the kitchen was about six feet above grade level, mahogany decking with an understructure of pressure-treated wood was installed to connect and blend with the terrace. Over time, it has weathered to a silvery gray that complements the flagstone.

The pool, just below the retaining wall and across a resurfaced gravel driveway, was also rejuvenated. The original bull-nose coping and a border of unattractive tile were replaced with flagstone, which helps harmonize the pool with the terrace above. Since the pool was surrounded by grass, which appealed neither to swimmers nor to sitters, a paved area was added on one side. Made of brick mortared in concrete, this terrace follows the curve of the pool in a kind of basketweave pattern. The warm terracotta color of the brick and its rough texture, combined with the terrace's intricate design, provide more visual interest than, and a pleasing change from, the flagstone surfaces.

It was the trelliswork that supplied the missing cohesive element and the major design interest in the yard. Lattice fencing, was placed at a height of six feet to screen the flagstone terrace from neighbors and four feet to enclose the swimming pool. In addition, a lattice pergola was constructed to connect the pool area with the guest house adjacent to the tennis court. Both ornamental and functional, the latticed structures achieved the desired harmony and privacy without blocking air, light, or views.

Planting materials supplied the final unifying detail. Trees, shrubs, ground covers, and vines that would be an integral part of the landscape structure were specified. For the perennial beds, a garden designer made selections that assured continuous and prolific flowers and foliage throughout the summer. The terrace garden was filled with pink pansies, white daffodils, and blue

In a basic palette of pastels, the perennials have a cooling, soothing effect on a hot summer day. Astilbe and daylilies (opposite, top) will bring a bit of outdoor color inside. Vigorous honeysuckle softens the look of the retaining wall (opposite, middle). The blocks of gray are the perfect foil for the daylilies and astilbe that bloom at their base.

The white-stained pool fencing also makes a decorative backdrop for showy perennials such as delphinium, monarda, and lythrum (opposite, bottom).

Replicas of old estate furniture from Maine enhance the flagstone terrace (right). Lacquered in white, the mahogany pieces hold up well in all kinds of weather and do not need to be brought indoors during the winter. Clematis, ivy, and climbing hydrangea will provide more shade as they grow up the trelliswork pergola outside the kitchen entrance.

A path of compacted stone dust leads from the driveway to the pool. It forms a pleasing border to the lush flowers along the fence.

anemones for springtime pleasure. They are followed by a mix of daylilies that bloom throughout the season in pale peach, pink, salmon, yellow, and deep burgundy for accent. Lavender, ceratostigma, and campanula edge the beds in soft blue-violet hues.

The garden by the pool echoes the one above, with some additions. They include delphinium, shasta daisy, Rudbeckia "Goldsturm," monarda, stokesia, lythrum "Morden's Pink," platycodon, astilbe, dicentra, phlox "Bright Eyes," nepeta, veronica, coreopsis "Moonbeam," geranium "lancastriense," and sedum "Autumn Joy." Shrub-like roses called "The Fairy," in soft pink, and "Goldflame" honeysuckle were planted to cascade over the retaining wall. Climbing hydrangea, clematis, silver lace, and honeysuckle are being trained up the latticework structures.

As a testimony to the success of its redesign, this vacation hideaway has become the owners' primary residence.

A dramatic focal point in the yard, the airy pergola (opposite) connects the pool terrace with the guest house. The see-through peaked roof provides filtered sunlight for the white violets, lamium, astilbes, hostas, and ferns that border the stone-dust path, which packs solid as it wears. The grid side walls serve as a trellis for clematis.

Replacing the old cement coping with flagstone has given the swimming pool (above) a fresh new look. For design continuity, the brick terrace repeats the graceful end curve. The old stone wall is left over from estate days. Of solid resin that looks like wood, the bright white furniture with blue-and-white striped cushions provides comfortable, carefree seating. Alberta spruces in terracotta pots flank the entrance to the pool house. Pink tree geraniums and blue-violet nierembergia help define the terrace border and supply splashes of color.

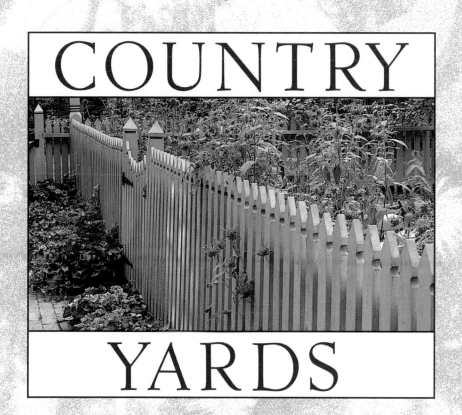

COUNTRY

YARDS

COLONIAL

GARDEN

The cedar clapboard exterior of the house (left) suits its rustic surroundings, as do the brick path and stone steps. The collection of stones placed throughout the property is one of many personal touches in the landscape. Pachysandra, azalea, laurel, holly, rhododendron, and euonymus thrive in the partly shaded front yard. A stand of irises (above) adds a striking accent to the understated fence.

No yard has more impact than one that strongly reflects the personality of its owners. The stamp of individuality is clearly seen in this herb garden and its surroundings, which are part of a one-and-a-half-acre site on a country road. Actively involved in the construction of their house when it was built, the owners were responsible for the Cape Cod design; the husband did some of the exterior and interior work himself. After they had lived in the house for a while, it was natural that their thoughts turned to taming their wooded land.

The wife thought of an herb garden, for she felt that the ordered, traditional character of this type of garden would be appropriate next to the eighteenth-century-style house. The couple chose a flat area on the north side of the house as the location for the new garden, which required the removal of some trees.

After the owners rotary tilled the 27 by 20 foot plot, they laid out the 4-foot wide paths for the garden's symmetrical plan, consisting of four corner beds and a central circle. Extra soil was added to the planting beds to raise their level slightly. Then they were enriched with equal amounts of top soil, peat moss, and sand for drainage. The paths were filled with sand, which served as the bed for the bricks that would later be added, without mortar, along with the walkway to a backyard perennial border, vegetable garden, and deck. The bricks, Boston City Hall pavers, are of a soft, rosy-gray hue that sets off the herbs beautifully. Pea gravel and crushed shells were other options for the walkways, but the brick's formal nature seemed more suitable. Finally, flat stepping stones were added within the large herb beds to enable the owners to reach the back of the garden without packing down the soil with their feet.

Spade-shaped tops on the pickets enclosing the herb garden and pyramidal end posts add design interest to the 40-inch-high fence that one of the owners handcrafted from common lumber. Instead of the customary white, the wood was finished in a sand-colored opaque stain, to complement the brick and the beige trim on the cedar clapboard house.

The herb garden was planted in stages. To begin the design, artemisia was planted in each corner and in the center circle. Borders of low-growing lamb's ears were added to anchor the long paths, ever-bearing alpine strawberries to the short ones. Lemon, silver, and wooly thyme were planted to fill the borders surrounding the curved path, and at the core of the central bed a long-stemmed yellow hybrid rose, "Apollo," reigns supreme. Forming the framework of the garden, these plants have been supplemented through the years by scented geraniums and lavender, pineapple sage, apple mint, French tarragon, bee balm, globe thistle, yarrow, rosemary, bay, oregano, basil, and parsley. Some are perennials, others are annuals that are planted in the spring to fill empty pockets and to provide seasonal change. Sometimes the owners add alyssum, nasturtiums, or calendula, which, because they are low-growing and bloom profusely, strike harmonious notes in an herb garden.

Geraniums planted among the English ivy add annual color outside the fence along the path leading to the garden gate and backyard. Also outside the fence, by the parking area, a tall climbing rose, "Coral Dawn," has been trained up the pickets to screen the garden from the road.

The owners do not even try to use all the herbs they grow. They enjoy their garden for many different reasons, both aesthetic and utilitarian. Not only is the garden a constant source of visual pleasure, with its varied textures, hues, and shapes, but it also has a pleasant aroma. And, of course, many of the herbs can be harvested

A small porch linking the house and garage (opposite) is an intimate spot for morning coffee. The bench is a larger version of one in the garden. Blending with the house and garden, a Colonial-style lamppost (top) was planned as part of the fence design. A walkway (middle) leads from the parking area to the garden gate and on to the backyard. Globe thistle blooms in the corner next to the lamppost. Its steel-blue flowers make lovely dried arrangements. The posts and finials on the back-porch railing (below) echo those on the garden fence, uniting house and yard.

One of the beauties of a picket fence is that, while marking boundaries, it does not completely close off one area from another. Here, the pink bee balm growing between the pickets and the geranium outside the fence link garden and yard. As seen here, pickets can double as stakes for tall plants. The colorful flowers look striking against the neutral beige of the fence.

for cooking (oregano, basil, tarragon, and so on), drying (rosemary, bay, oregano, lavender), and making sweet-scented bouquets for the house (lavender and rosemary). The owner-gardener likes to give plants away when she divides and replants some of them in the spring, and she likes to start new cuttings that are gifts from friends.

In addition, the owners find the upkeep of their garden to be relatively undemanding, for herbs are easy to grow and need little care. An herb garden is a rewarding choice for people who don't have a lot of time to devote to gardening.

The symmetrical geometric pattern of the brick walkways gives the garden a formal, eighteenth-century aspect (above). The profusion of plants, creeping over the edges of their beds, and the wood-and-iron bench, an ideal place to rest and enjoy the beauty and fragrance of the herbs, add a more casual, inviting note. The abundance of plants is a lush foil to the spare exterior of the house (opposite, above). The Williamsburg

ball-and-chain latch (opposite, below left) is appropriate in the Colonial setting, and makes the gate close with an appealing click. The herbs are cut for cooking, drying, or making bouquets (opposite, below right). The owners use them as their mood dictates—or, they simply enjoy the fragrance and beauty of the herbs in their natural state.

ART
MEETS NATURE

The successful fusion of sophisticated design and raw nature gives this one-acre waterfront property its unique spirit. The design is the result of a close collaboration between architect Steven Haas and landscape architect Randolph Marshall. Part of an old estate that had been broken up into building lots, the spectacular piece of land that provided their raw material had a 200-foot frontage on Long Island Sound with a 23-foot elevation that ensured the building site's safety during severe storms.

When the owners bought the property, it also had an expanse of lawn extending to an ugly concrete sea wall. Besides being somewhat inappropriate for the rocky shoreline, the grass was killed by the salt spray. Moreover, the lawn attracted Canada geese, which liked to eat the grass seed when the area was re-seeded. One of the owners' first priorities, therefore, was to restore the waterfront to its original state and to substitute indigenous seaside plantings for the lawn. In addition, they wanted a glass-walled house with all major rooms located at the rear to capitalize on the panoramic views. The front of the house, on the other hand, was to be more conventional, with a suburban blend of play spaces and entertainment areas.

First to go was the old sea wall. After it was removed, the remaining earth was power-washed away to expose the natural rock along the shore. New boulders were brought in to augment those that were there, and new retaining walls were built in organic, rounded shapes that conformed to the rocky terrain. The walls were used to retain new soil for planting beds surrounding a walkway to two decks at the tide line 60 feet away from the house, and to fashion a small, sheltered sandy beach area. Built from granite that came from a highway project, the retaining walls were mortared with reinforcing rods to withstand the forces of wind and water. The two decks were built on steel frames, which were drilled and cemented into the rocks.

Because of the unified design concept and the coordination between Haas and Marshall, the house, walks, decks, and landscaping have a subtle harmony. Reminiscent of the Bauhaus style, the house was designed with low, horizontal lines. Even the serpentine walls of glass on the rear were mullioned in wide horizontal bands. The neutral-density tinted glass removes brightness and glare, but does not alter natural colors. From the beach areas, the window walls become murals as they reflect the seaside vegetation. Because the living room, dining room, kitchen, and bedrooms were all placed on this northeast elevation to overlook the water vistas and the seaside plantings, there is a consistency and harmony indoors as

To restore the shoreline to its natural, rockbound state (right) required the removal of a sea wall and lawn. The glass-walled house mirrors the ornamental grasses, *rosa rugosa*, and other seaside plantings (opposite) that are in character with the seaside setting. From inside the house, the plantings look like a rich tapestry of subtle hues, shapes, and textures.

well as out. Rooftop decks, accessible from the bedrooms, provide private sitting and more viewing areas in the open air.

All the materials for the house and landscape were chosen for their rugged, complementary characteristics and for their resistance to the vicissitudes of nature—salt-water spray, wind, storms, and hot sun. The cedar siding on the house's exterior was finished in a longlasting gray stain, which was enlivened by aluminum window mullions painted light green. Slate and granite were used for upper walks, and teak for the boardwalk to the shore and for the two decks. (Long used in ship construction, teak is especially practical in a salt-water environment.) Because of ground shifts and the pressure of the water, the boardwalk was built on a concrete and stone foundation. Narrow wood strips, about 1⅝ inches wide, were

The contrast between the sheltered, parklike front yard (opposite, above and below) and the open, wild environment in the back lends excitement to the landscape plan and provides two totally different moods for outdoor activities. The front yard is used for family fun and entertaining. New sod supplies a soft carpet of green for the children's play structures, which are the same sturdy play equipment as that used in national parks. A croquet court and a badminton court are available for the grown-ups. A small orchard (opposite, below) offers a delightful backdrop—and snack—for the players. The painted mahogany furniture makes handsome landscape accessories. In the backyard, the paths, steps, and retaining walls conform to the rugged terrain. Many different sedums, grasses, and low-growing evergreens flank the granite stepping stones that lead from the house to the teak boardwalk (top, near right). Honeysuckle softens the stone retaining wall (top, far right). Teak walkways (middle, near and far right; bottom, near right) lead to the decks. Lights built into the steps and placed among the plants assure safe footing at night. Rough-hewn steps (bottom, far right) lead to the beach.

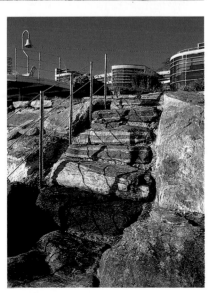

screwed together and pegged with teak dowels, giving the steps, risers, and landings a pleasant undulating flow.

The two circular platforms that jut out over the shoreline like the decks of ships were built to conform to the natural rock formations. One is 16 feet in diameter, and the other, used for barbecuing, is 20 feet. The railings for the decks and for stone steps leading down to the beach were constructed, like those on ships, of stainless steel and white vinyl-covered rope. To eliminate the job of battening-down the hatches on windy, stormy days, the furniture is permanently affixed to the teak decking with stainless steel thumbscrews. All the teak was finished with oil, which holds up well in moisture and sun, but must be reapplied every year.

The seaside landscaping was designed to be a subtle tapestry of colors, textures, and shapes rather than picturebook flower beds. The plantings are scaled so as not to block any views. A variety of ornamental grasses—pampas, plume, fountain, maiden, ribbon, cord, and zebra—create striking accents with their graceful, arching forms, swirling foliage, and feathery blooms. Ever-changing as the seasons progress, they provide indestructible visual pleasure year-round. Also surrounding the boardwalk are Russian olive, *rosa rugosa*, bamboo, pigmy barberry, many different kinds of sedum, and such ground-hugging evergreens as Bar Harbor juniper, procumbens juniper, and mugo pine. Honeysuckle cascades gracefully over the retaining walls.

The front yard was designed in a completely different mood. Manicured and sheltered, it was given a new sod lawn and an in-ground sprinkler system. Play equipment was included for two young children and their friends. For the adults and their guests, a croquet court and a badminton court encourage exercise and amusement. Bent grass, which is used for putting greens, was planted for the croquet playing field, since it can be kept closely cropped (it needs to be cut every few days). Also part of this parklike setting are a small orchard of dwarf apple and pear trees and painted mahogany furniture that was reproduced from pieces in London's Hyde Park. The bench, table, and chairs remain outdoors year-round, but they need repainting every two or three years to keep them protected from the elements.

Nestled among the rocks at the tide line, the two decks afford much pleasure during the summer with their expansive views of Long Island Sound. The oiled teak decking, vinyl-coated railings, and permanently anchored furniture evoke the feeling of being on a boat.

On the upper deck (near right, above and below), a gas barbecue and sink are at hand for family cookouts and entertaining. The bell-shaped post light is a replica of the gas lamps used along the old Camino Real when California was Spanish territory. With the granite retaining wall as a rugged backdrop, the new sandy cove (far right) is an ideal spot for sunbathing and catnapping. Storage closets set into the rocks house a refrigerator, beach paraphernalia, and a sailboat mast.

Adorning the perimeter and screening the yard from the neighbors is a mix of Japanese black pine, Canadian hemlock, blue spruce, and Douglas fir. The plantings decrease in scale as they approach the house, with a middle level of native and hybrid rhododendrons, azaleas, holly, and andromeda. For border beds, such perennials as peonies, daylilies, astilbe, iris, and hosta provide summer interest. Annuals such as begonias, impatiens, ageratum, and marigolds are planted in May to supply more color.

Keeping the cultivated and wild areas of this seaside property under control requires an enormous amount of work and is left up to professionals. However, all the mowing, pruning, trimming, weeding, and planting pay off handsomely, as this distinctive intermingling of natural and manmade elements shows.

PONDSIDE

RENOVATION

What attracted architect-owner Peter Woerner to his picture-postcard property was the quality of the sunlight and the large pond, which had once fed a local granite quarry.

An old farmhouse that originally belonged to the widow of the quarry master was still standing, and, though not suitable for Woerner's needs, it became the nucleus of a lovely melding of architectural and landscaping elements. The architect demolished most of the outdated structure, but he did preserve the framework, around which he designed a three level, contemporary house in the vernacular of the area. He also added 14 feet to the south end of the house facing the pond to obtain space for a master bedroom and balcony on the top level, a dining room and adjacent kitchen on the main middle level, and guest quarters on the bottom level. In addition, a deck, with a storage room below, was built off the dining room for warm-weather meals by the water. The angled shape of the deck was determined by an old quarry road that was turned into a grassy waterside walkway.

Because Woerner needed a studio and wanted a garage at the main living level, he decided to combine the two in a single building, which he set into the hillside at a right angle to the farmhouse. It was the juxtaposition of these two structures that delineated his outdoor spaces.

Built into the sloping terrain near the water, the deck blends well with the pastoral scene. This spacious outdoor room is accessible from the dining area and from the lawn, and it provides an idyllic outdoor room, day or night, for sipping wine and viewing pond life.

A storage room with an outdoor entrance (opposite, above) is built below the deck.

The roofed add-on (opposite, below) helps keep the wood dry.

The angled shape of the deck follows the outline of the walkway—originally an old quarry road—that leads to the water (opposite, below right).

Located in a small section of a wall connecting the house and the studio, the doorway with an arched lintel (right) adds a decorative, whimsical detail. Leading from one courtyard to the other, the doorway functions like a gate in a fence.

A successful merging of architecture
and landscape, the garden courtyard
is nestled into the right angle formed
by the windowed end wall of the new
studio-garage building, the side wall
of the den in the remodeled farmhouse, and the huge blocks of pink
granite used for the retaining walls.
Locally quarried blocks of granite
form the rugged retaining wall for the
grass-covered garden courtyard.
In the terraced planting beds,
roses and a variety of perennials
provide colorful blooms throughout
the summer.

The pond is the major focus of the landscape. Not only can it be enjoyed from a deck off the dining room and a deck off the master bedroom, but the owner-architect likes to fish and canoe in its tranquil waters. The 18-foot-high railing of the dining deck (opposite, above) serves as a bench and as a tabletop.

The steel railing on the deck off the master bedroom (opposite, below left) is painted in an earthy terracotta to blend easily with the weathered fir decking and with the surrounding greenery.

Steps from the dining deck (opposite, below right) lead to the storage room below and to the pond.

Originally, the approach to the house was from above, with the land sloping toward the pond. The inclined terrain was altered to create two courtyards, which were enclosed with retaining walls built of huge random blocks of pink granite indigenous to the area. To stabilize the dry-set walls, chinks of stone were fitted into the cracks. One of the courtyards, which has easy access to the garage and the house, was paved in ⅜ inch of red tipple stone over a compacted driveway base and became an entrance for cars. The other, a garden courtyard, was given a more intimate, cloistered feeling. It is covered in grass with terraced planting beds, and is accessible from a den and from the main entrance court. It is also visible from the oversized windows on the studio's gabled end wall. (These windows were stock industrial steel sash windows that the architect modified to achieve a bright interior with expansive views of the outdoors.)

The tiered garden, in an English cottage style, became the focal point of the landscape. It was planted with old-fashioned pink and white rosebushes in the background and a variety of perennials in the foreground. Aside from these plantings, Woerner preserved the unspoiled beauty of the property. His choice of materials and finishes strengthened the rustic character of the land. In addition to the extensive use of stone for retaining walls throughout the site, the house was clad in red cedar shingles that were left to weather naturally. However, for a simple look, the gabled end wall of the studio, facing the garden court, was surfaced in vertical cedar siding. For design continuity, vertical exterior surfaces of the deck were also shingled. Vertical grain Douglas fir, finished with a clear preservative, was used for the decking itself. All the woods have mellowed to a compatible silver-gray.

The architect's restrained handling of the farmland and the barnlike buildings—his respect for the terrain and use of unfinished wood and stone—echoes the rustic setting of this property and shows a consideration for the past and for the spirit of the countryside.

HISTORIC

HERB GARDEN

When Ragna Tischler Goddard and her husband Tom purchased an eighteenth-century farmhouse on six acres of land, she began to research the architecture of the house with a view toward its restoration. Her studies aroused an interest in plantings of the period, and she soon realized that the restoration would not be complete unless the grounds, which were overgrown and poorly drained, were designed in an authentic manner as well. The three formal herb gardens that resulted offer valuable lessons in historical design.

With her background in art and botany and her strong sense of history, it was not surprising that the owner should design the gardens in the formal seventeenth- and eighteenth-century style, rather than with today's natural, informal approach. Historically, gardens were meant to be extensions of house, with walks, beds, and a central focus—in the old days a water source—and that is how the landscaping here was conceived.

The layout for all three gardens—a main, sundial garden, a topiary garden, and a knot garden—was based on a plan that is five thousand years old. The layout features two major walks intersecting each other to form a cross, with other walkways radiating from a central focal point. In the Goddards' gardens, a sundial in the main garden, a fountain in the topiary garden, and a statue of a floral bouquet in the knot garden replaced the ancient cistern that was the historical focal point, but they are nonetheless universal symbols of life, like the cistern. The gardens are arranged on the property to form three corners of a square, with the house forming the fourth corner. The central focus of each garden is visible through archways in the garden next to it. The kitchen door of the

house leads to the topiary garden, and the front door opens to the knot garden. The main sundial garden is accessible through the other two gardens.

Interestingly—and with historical accuracy—an old grape arbor that had collapsed from the weight of one-hundred-year-old plants became the orientation point for the sundial garden, which was the first to be developed. The old arbor structure was resurrected and the vines rejuvenated. The arbor serves not only as a divider between the main garden and the topiary garden, but as an

A trio of herb gardens creates an authentic setting for the eighteenth-century farmhouse (opposite). Massive granite stepping stones lead from the front door across a crushed-stone walkway to the knot garden. A profusion of blooms and foliage (above) adds an untamed note to the overall formal setting.

axis leading from one to the other. It was aligned with the fountain and the sundial, as well as with the gabled roof line of the house (which runs in the same north-south direction), creating a further link between the architecture of the house and the gardens.

The 50-by-100-foot sundial garden was designed in an eighteenth-century style, with more than twenty raised beds of fragrant, culinary, and medicinal herbs. Among them are lemon-scented creeping thyme, lavender, camphor-scented southernwood, American mountain mint, French tarragon, winter savory, ambrosia, marjoram, Russian sage, agrimony, germander, horehound, epazote, great burnet, false indigo, tansy, and Egyptian onion. A picket fence defines the long north border that separates the main and knot gardens; the boundary line on the south side is a solid board fence.

Because the land was boggy and water built up during the spring thaws and heavy rains, it was necessary to build a drainage ditch inside the herb garden. Ragna Goddard hand-dug the ditch to a depth of one and a half feet and lined it with fieldstone. The garden's brick paths were laid with slightly crested centers to allow for runoff. Also, as they settled, the spaces tightened between the bricks, and the walks became more stable and resistant to frost heaves. The grape arbor was underplanted with sweet woodruff and columbine.

The 50-by-50-foot topiary garden was designed according to the traditions of ancient Egypt and seventeenth-century France. It was enclosed by 3-foot-high L-shaped stone walls, which created a sheltered, sunken atmosphere for a quiet, meditative retreat. Tom Goddard dry-set the walls with granite boulders found on the property. (He was, in fact, responsible for all the stonework around the house.) The fountain at the garden's core was designed and built by Ragna Goddard from different commercial parts, including seats from garden benches and pedestals from sundials. Two pumps recirculate the water from the top and from the sides. A Renaissance-inspired fountain on the back fence, at the rear end of the grape arbor, provides another focal point. Besides the junipers and boxwoods, which are the backbone of the topiary garden, English ivy spills over the fountain walls. Silver mound, santolina, and prostrate rosemary supply subtle color and textural contrasts. The sides of trellised arch to the garden are covered with a fragrant climbing rose called *Rosa gallica officianalis*, which was popular in the thirteenth century and is one of the oldest roses known.

The 35-by-17-foot knot garden, the smallest of the three, was inspired by motifs from Persia and Tudor England. It was designed with a 12-foot-square center bed of interlocking low hedges in the form of a knot and two side beds, 5 feet wide each. Woolly thyme, thrift, germander, rue, lamb's-ear, and circle onion were planted to form the decorative knot. The side beds comprise perennial flax, silver horehound, and silver-leaved speedwell, accented by four chubby upright junipers. A graceful trellis with an arch provides a backdrop for the knot garden and also leads the eye toward a birch forest in the distance.

Connecting the knot garden and the main sundial garden is an arbor formed by pleached Seckel pear trees. In the technique of pleaching, which is used to create arches or arbors without any supports, the branches of a double row of trees are intertwined, pruned, and trained to form a canopy. Initially, the trees are coaxed into shape with string, but eventually they will support each other and stand alone.

All the fences, walls, walks, arches, and plantings in the gardens were carefully planned to relate to each other, with the varying

Boxwood and standards are used effectively to delineate entrances and borders. Urns of rosemary and sweet bay (above) stand guard at the entrance to the knot garden. They are brought indoors during the winter. Walls and walks of rough-cut granite are perfect foils for the varied foliage of the different herbs and shrubs.

'Blue beauty' rue, germander, and thrift, filled in with lamb's-ear and circle onion, form the decorative pattern in the center bed of the knot garden (opposite). Wichita Blue junipers provide height and year-round interest at the sides. Beyond the arched trellis at the rear of the knot garden, a park-like area is being developed.

The drainage ditch in the main garden (above) was dug by hand by one of the owners, who then lined it with fieldstone. Oriental poppies and columbines are among the perennials that add color to the sundial garden (right). The gateway in the picket fence (opposite) forms a symmetrical frame for the floral sculpture that is the focus of the knot garden. The pear-tree arbor was created by the ancient training technique known as pleaching.

horizontals and verticals supplying scale, proportion, and depth. All the herb beds were raised, not only for aesthetic reasons but for drainage as well. Most of the plantings are low and in subtle shades of greens, with splashes of seasonal color. Shapes and sizes were selected for three layers: such edging plants as boxwood, germander, winter savory, and lavender are one layer; ground covers such as creeping thyme, veronica, and ajuga form the second; and the third is made of accent plants, such as the junipers, boxwoods, and standards of myrtle, rosemary, and sweet bay. (Standards are plants that have been trained by taking off all the side branches and allowing the top to bush out.) Placed at garden entrances and at the corners of garden beds, the accent plants draw the eye into the gardens and create depth. Also, along with the boxwoods, which

are used extensively throughout the project, they supply a sense of constancy and permanence. Both the sundial and topiary gardens have patches of shade and places to sit. To keep weeds under control, all the paths and garden beds were covered with landscape fabric, which allows light and air to penetrate. The herb beds were also covered with a thin layer of crushed shale for mulch. (Because herbs do not like rich soil, no organic mulch was needed.)

Gardeners who consider these gardens too time-consuming and difficult to create can at least see them, for the Goddards have turned what was a pleasurable pasttime into a business venture called The Sundial Herb Garden. Visitors can walk through the gardens, learn about herbs, drink herbal teas, and buy a variety of herbal products.

The Sundial Herb Garden is the collective name for the three classically styled gardens that belong to Ragna and Tom Goddard and which they share with the public for tours, teas, and herb lore. The arbor of pleached Seckel pear trees leads from the knot garden through an opening in the picket fence to the main garden flanked by high box hedges. Hibiscus trees and purple-plumed gay feather add splashes of color along the fence. Low boxwood borders the brick walks.

With its ornate fountain, stone walls, and backdrop of dense evergreens, the topiary garden has a secluded atmosphere for quiet contemplation. It is distinguished by boxwood and juniper trimmed in topiary shapes. Entry to the garden is through a trellised arch flanked by olive-tree standards (near right and below). A climbing apothecary rose (*Rosa gallica officianalis*) adds scent and decoration. The wall fountain, with cherubs and a vineyard motif (far right) is a focal point at the far end of the old grape arbor.

UPDATED

TRADITION

The owners of this property, less than two acres in scrub-oak woods, turned bare land, with no electricity, no water, and only a dirt road connecting their wilderness to civilization, into a sophisticated blend of traditional and modern landscape design. Their dream included a house that would be architecturally compatible with others in the area, a large deck for entertaining, and a swimming pool. In starting such a project from scratch, they had not only to clear the land to yield a sunny southern exposure, but also to overcome the steep slope of the property. The slope was managed with the creation, in essence, of two terraced sections, formed by the deck and a rock garden, that also ease the transition from house to pool.

Situated on the highest point of ground, the house—in the Colonial style, but updated for today's needs—blends well with neighboring homes. The dark gray clapboard siding contrasts with the white trim. Modern floor-to-ceiling windows fill the house with light, creating a close indoor-outdoor relationship.

To further link the present with the past, the spacious deck sports an old-fashioned, porch railing instead of today's popular built-in benches. The white of the railing not only unites the deck with the house, but provides a foil for the silvery-gray deck and teak furniture. Built from durable cedar and finished with a clear wood preservative, the deck has developed a weathered patina naturally.

An ideal solution for the difficult slope, the rock garden, with its mix of soft and hard forms, provides a pleasing transition from the deck to the lawn below. Topsoil was brought in for the plantings but the rocks came from the ground excavated for the pool. They were strategically positioned to help hold the earth and to provide

The somewhat spare exterior of the house (opposite) is softened by the brick steps and by the hedges and flowers that welcome the visitor. Both the doorway and the entrance path are Colonial in style. An easy-care gravel driveway (above) widens into a parking area. The gate allows entry into the backyard without going through the house.

pockets for the plants, which include candytuft, lavender, thyme, and silver-mound artemisia.

New brick, used for the steps, walkway, and pool surround, is a leitmotif, unifying different elements of the yard. Laid in a stack and running bond pattern, the brick has the look of old paving with a soft, rosy texture that complements the greens and pinks that predominate in the garden. In the steps, a collection of old bricks cast with the names of the manufacturers was interspersed with the new ones, adding visual interest and a sense of history. The Gunite pool is not quite a classic rectangle, since graceful curves soften both ends of the 40-by-18-foot pool. Brick coping and decking add another traditional note.

To meet building codes, a 6-foot-high chain-link fence surrounds the property line by the pool. Painted green, it "disappears" into the woods, as do the posts, which are spray-painted black. Latticework fences at other boundaries, at once decorative and practical, offer privacy without blocking air or views, and they provide a backdrop for perennial beds and support for climbing roses. Elsewhere on the property, latticework is used effectively to screen pool equipment and an air-conditioner motor.

The yard's warm personality is largely due to the husband's enthusiasm and personal involvement in all the planning phases. He is a dedicated gardener with a particular love of roses. Indeed, roses are a dominant landscape feature. More than fifty varieties of hybrid teas, floribundas, grandifloras, and climbers, in a subtle pale pink and white palette, bloom continuously from early spring until frost, adding to the aura of yesteryear. The wife, an artist who exhibits at a nearby gallery, paints the flowers her husband plants.

Although the selection, placement, and care of the roses are the special province of the owner, Long Island landscape gardener Lisa Stamm is responsible for the rock garden and perennial beds, planted for four-season enjoyment. Slow-growing dwarf evergreens, weeping cherry, Japanese maple, and ornamental grass provide the backdrop for perennials, bulbs, and annuals that supply spring and summer color.

The white and gray of the deck (top) echo the colors of the house, while the climbing roses add color to the scene with a pink that is reminiscent of the brick paths and steps. This view of brick steps (above) shows how the property was terraced to break up the steep slope. Lighting on the stairs ensures that the descent is safe as well as smooth. A large stand of ornamental grasses (right) adds drama to the rock garden, otherwise populated with low-growing and miniature plants.

Forming a strong yet graceful geometric pattern, the brick walkway and pool surround continue the Colonial theme introduced in the front of the house around to the backyard. The rounded ends and steps of the pool also add a bit of fancy to the standard rectangular shape.

The table, chairs, and umbrella (opposite) match those on the deck. Teak furniture can withstand the moisture and salt air that characterize the near-coastal property. A garden bench (above) set well away from the pool and deck is a place of quiet respite. The pool equipment is screened from view by a lattice-covered wall (right) adorned with some of the owner's beloved roses. A similar structure hides an air-conditioner motor elsewhere on the property.

YARD

WITH A VIEW

A small, undistinguished vacation cottage sat on a 4-acre site 30 feet above the Long Island Sound when a conservation-oriented couple bought it in the late 1970s. Yet even though the 1940s house itself was inadequate, and overgrown vegetation blocked views of the water, they were able to see the potential of the dramatic setting.

Because the husband and wife were concerned with the environment, preservation of the natural surroundings was paramount in their planning. They turned to architect Peter Woerner, whose seaside home they knew and admired, to help them refashion the simple summer house into a comfortable year-round residence. The structure was remodeled inside and out. In addition to new windows, doors, roof, and shingled siding, a glassed-in porch was added to the east side facing the water, and a greenhouse expanded space on the south side.

The greenhouse was designed as a work area for the wife, Ellen Ebersole, who is a landscape designer, and as a bright, sunny extension of the family's living space that could be enjoyed particularly in the cold winter months.

For warm-weather pleasure, Woerner provided two outdoor sitting areas. An east-facing deck was built around a maple tree that supplies welcome shade in the summer. Fitting neatly into the L-shape of the house, the deck, which was set on piers and sided in cedar shingles, echoes the house in both materials and design. It was styled with cutouts below the combination bench-railings to allevi-

The repetition of design and materials makes the cedar-clad deck (opposite) an integral part of the house structure. Built-in benches supplement other seating and give the deck a neat, uncluttered appearance.

Fieldstone not only provides a transition from deck to yard (above), but it links lawn, deck, and stone retaining wall.

The fiery red orchid, with its long trailing branches (left), is another indoor plant that lends a decorative touch to the deck during warm-weather months.

The fir deck and fieldstone landing provide pleasing backdrops for a collection of jade plants and other succulents that spend their summers outdoors and their winters in the greenhouse(top and above).

To break up the expanse of the landing, mother-of-thyme is encouraged to creep along the crevices between the fieldstone (above).

ate any feeling of being boxed in. Durable, knotless Douglas fir was used for the decking. (The wood was treated with a clear preservative which is renewed every few years.) At the base of broad steps leading to the lawn, a fieldstone landing was added to improve drainage and eliminate a low spot that got muddy during wet weather. The stone, found on the property, was laid in 4 inches of sand; it makes a pleasant transition from the deck to the lawn.

The second sitting area was placed next to a large boulder that had been part of the original terrain, and other native stones were positioned to define the free-form shape of the 15-by-20-foot terrace. The terrace was paved in a local beige-gray decorative stone laid on a base of compacted stone-dust and gravel approximately 6 inches thick.

In order to open up vistas, it was necessary to remove some trees and shrubs. (Some had already been cleared away as the result of a hurricane and drought.) Otherwise, the basic land form and indigenous vegetation, such as the red cedars, staghorn sumac, bayberry, and meadow grasses, were not touched. Paths were mowed through the grasses for access to the beach and water.

Ellen Ebersole chose new planting materials that would not distract from the view and that would be able to withstand the rigorous seaside conditions. Tolerance to wind, drought, and salt was a critical consideration, as was minimal maintenance, which partly meant conserving the property's well water as much as possible. Daylilies predominate in pale pink, peach, and yellow hues. The pastel palette was deliberately selected not to compete with the vista, and to complement the weathered woods, grasses, and fieldstone. Yarrow, hybrid mullein, and sea holly were also planted for their low-maintenance characteristics. In the spring, such shrubs as broom and mock orange supply additional color. In addition, old apple trees flower in pale pink and white, with daffodils blooming freely below them.

Both the indoor and outdoor spaces of this revitalized property are in close harmony with nature, a fact that must give its environmentally conscious owners as much satisfaction as does the wondrous view they enjoy throughout the year.

A grass path (left) meanders through the indigenous red cedars, sumac, meadow grasses, and an old apple orchard on its way down to the shoreline 30 feet below. The day-lilies, furniture, and stone terrace (above) are in neutral hues that do not take away from the beauty of the natural vegetation and the views of the water.

COURTYARD ARTISTRY

Two acres of reclaimed farmland bordering a protected wetlands is the enticing site for a yard that clearly shows the hands and hearts of its artist owners, Margaret Kerr and Robert Richenburg. When they moved here, the couple was irresistably drawn to the flat land and to the angular house that rested so comfortably on it. The sun-drenched property affords expansive views of the sky, marshes, water, and wildlife. The cedar-clad house, with its multiple shed roofs, is an updated version of the shingled farmhouses that dotted the landscape over two hundred years ago.

The owners had no desire to change the house's contemporary structure. Built on five levels with an open-plan interior, it was designed by architect Peter Price as part of a compound that also included a detached garage, a swimming pool, and a pool house. Nevertheless, though the vistas were compelling and the grounds were embellished with stands of sculpture-like cedar trees, the couple did feel the lack of a cultivated garden and of any points of personal interest.

They ultimately decided to create a more or less formal courtyard. As happens with creative people and with garden projects, one thing led to another. Margaret Kerr's deep interest in plants and in medieval art prompted the creation of a garden filled with herbs that were grown in the Middle Ages and the decision to include at the garden's core a lily pool with a fountain, as was common in medieval times. In addition, her special feeling for old brick easily led to the selection of this time-honored material for the paths between the planting beds.

Blossoming santolina and lavender (above) are two of the hundreds of medieval herbs whose selection was inspired by those grown at the Cloisters in New York City. The weathered gray cedar siding, rosy brick hues, and green foliage of the various herbs (opposite) offer a subtle mix of materials, colors, textures, and shapes, particularly when viewed against a bright blue sky.

Enclosed by the house, artists' studios, and the swimming pool, the herb garden (above) became a central courtyard with the ambience of another time. In order not to break up the flow of space, the lily pool was sunk into the ground instead of raised. The fountain-jet supplies a gently splashing sound all year long. Boards of weathered cedar fencing (left) are staggered to allow air to penetrate. Backed by espaliered pear trees and flanked by old-fashioned, romantic violets, the simple oak bench suits its surroundings. Mitered corners add interest to the pool's brick border (opposite, above and below). Goldfish and pots of hardy lilies winter over, but the tropical lilies need replacing every spring.

The first request the owners made of architect Price was to design a studio, linked to the house, where Richenburg, a painter and sculptor, could work. Once the studio was built, Kerr was free to figure out the correct proportions for the garden, which fit logically into a sunny 38-foot-by-26-foot space between the house and the swimming pool.

The construction of the garden was a combined effort, involving Kerr, now artist-turned-mason, her children, and a professional mason from the area. The lily pool went in first. A hole was dug with a backhoe; an 8-foot-square, 4-foot deep form with reinforcing rods was built; and concrete was poured. A drain was included to prevent any overflow, and a waterproof electric connection was installed for the fountain-jet and recirculating pump.

The garden paths were laid next. Their widths of 6 and 4 feet were modeled after those in the herb garden at the Cloisters, the medieval branch of The Metropolitan Museum of Art in New York City. To ensure a firm, weed-free base, a 5-inch bed of stone-dust was laid, then watered and flattened with a rented compactor until it became almost like concrete. The brick was set onto this base in a herringbone pattern. Sand was then swept into the cracks and the paving was edged with treated wood.

The remaining spaces of the courtyard were turned into a symmetrical arrangement of planting beds that were enriched with composted manure. Selected mostly for their historical and visual appeal, several hundred herbs, either authentic carryovers from medieval days or modern-day hybrids, now fill the garden with a mix of shapes, textures, colors, and scents. In each corner next to the pool, quince bushes are surrounded by winter savory and a variety of thymes. Other symbols of the Middle Ages include the Madonna lily, violets, lavender, santolina, lady's mantle, rue, lovage, tansy, lemon balm, angelica, costmary, and wormwood.

Artful design is evident not only in the overall structure of the courtyard, but in the thoughtful detailing. The pool, planned as a serene, quiet focal point for the garden, contains four pots of white lilies, two pots of hardy, day-blooming varieties, and two of night-blooming tropicals, which are particularly spectacular in moonlight. Goldfish supply a dash of color. To extend the feeling of the garden and to integrate it with the rest of the property, a pergola was designed to direct the eye and traffic toward a bronze statue by Jason Seley in the yard. Since the land slopes slightly here, broad, shallow steps composed of treated wood risers and creamy gravel

treads were built to accommodate the change of level. Other finishing touches include two oak benches inspired by examples at the Cloisters and two dwarf espaliered pear trees trained to grow horizontally in what is known as a "double cordon" pattern against the silver-gray cedar fence.

One might expect that by the end of the summer in which the garden was completed Kerr would not want to look at or handle another brick. But this did not happen. The project only increased her enthusiasm and appreciation for the material's potential, so much so that it inspired a unique new art form: "rugs" made from bricks. In order to work on these brick rugs, or site sculptures, Kerr added another studio to the compound. This one was sound-proofed, for the carefully selected bricks need to be machine-cut by an experienced masonry worker into small pieces of different shapes. For textural contrast, both the flat side and the edges of the brick are used to fashion the geometric designs of the rugs, which are influenced by the traditional patterns of old oriental rugs. The rugs are set in movable steel frames with holes in the bottom for drainage. The finished rugs, which have become accents throughout the landscape, can be removed for gallery shows.

Details can make the difference between the ordinary and the exceptional. Opening the courtyard to the landscape beyond, the pergola (above left), built from 4 by 4s of treated lumber, is embellished with wisteria vines in the center and climbing roses at the ends. Laid over landscape cloth to keep out weeds and aid drainage, the gravel-covered steps lead to the bronze sculpture and one of Margaret Kerr's many brick rugs, which are scattered throughout the yard (above and below, center). Made from different sizes and shapes of cut brick, these site sculptures play up the shadings and textures of the material. A espalier pear tree adorns one wall of the garage (above, right). In a single U form, the dwarf variety grows to about 15 inches wide and 5 to 6 feet high. These espaliers require at least six hours of full sun a day to blossom and set fruit.

Artist Robert Richenburg's interest in sculpture is seen in the "rock garden" that ornaments the pool decking (above and left). Some of the rocks in his collection are referred to as sculptures, others simply as "piles of stones." All supply pleasing shapes and textures against the weathered wood.

COMPLEX

SIMPLICITY

Pool planning involves specific considerations: Enclosures should be aesthetically pleasing while still meeting local codes, and siting should not interfere with views or dominate the landscape. The owners of this summer house presented these problems to architects Ben Benedict and Carl Pucci of BumpZoid. In addition, the husband wanted an uninterrupted sight line from the house to the river, the wife wanted to swim laps, and the three children wanted only to get wet and play water games. No one wanted the usual poolside plantings and seating.

Located on a creek that flows into the ocean, the vernacular shingle-style house was set far back from the bulkheaded beachfront. The lawn extended a hundred feet, then dipped down and flattened out again for another hundred feet to two boathouses.

The architects developed a simple, bold plan that both respected the flatness of the terrain and maintained the expansive vistas. The pool was placed where the two levels meet, built so that the surface of the water is approximately two feet above the lower lawn and two feet below the upper, thus creating an intermediary level. It was surrounded by grass, rather than a conventional patio. The grass was retained with a 2-foot-high brick wall that is invisible from the pool. To meet local safety ordinances, a 4-foot-high chain-link fence was installed all around the pool outside the retaining wall. However, the wall was cleverly concealed between 4-foot-high

privet hedges planted on either side of it. And because of the raised pool level, only two feet of hedge are visible from the pool. (The hedge is kept trimmed to this height.) Thus no views are blocked and no one feels trapped by a high enclosure.

The hedge and chain-link fence were interrupted on one long side of the pool for a niche that encloses a spa. The brick wall was built up and a curve added here. A round window was placed in the wall so that it would be possible to look through it from either above or below the pool level.

The entrance to the pool is like a promenade. A striking painted steel gate with a large glass oculus opens onto a small terrace that has steps down to the pool level and down again into the pool itself. The pool steps are sited in a cutout that breaks up the rigid 18-by-36-foot rectangle. Coping of Italian limestone enhances the dark gray plaster finish in the Gunite pool and assures a nonslippery surface when wet. Bent grass is used for the pool surround and continues the manicured look of the lower lawn level. Lighting is installed at regular intervals on the face of the brick wall. Reflecting off the edge of the hedge, the lighting outlines the entire area for nighttime use. A gate similar to that at the entrance opens through the hedge at the far end of the pool.

Because the owners did not want to sit by the pool, no umbrellas, furniture, or plantings interfere with the visual impact of the level landscape. Therefore, the design interest comes from form and architecture rather than from horticulture and garden accessories. For example, the brick wall and step risers match the house's foundation and other brick walls on the property. In addition, a geometric harmony is created by the pattern of the lights around

The pool area of the seaside property emphasizes structural rather than horticultural elements. The iron entry gate is painted deep red and adorned with an etched glass medallion that echoes the round window in the brick retaining wall that surrounds the spa. Coated in black, the chain-link fence disappears in the dense foliage of the privet hedge.

the pool and in the pool steps, by the squares of the pool coping and entry terrace, by the openwork of the teak chairs that sit at the terrace corners, and by the sea horizon motif etched in the gates.

Even the two existing boathouses became strong design elements in the yard. Although zoning laws did not permit any structural alterations, cosmetic changes were allowed. New siding and white trim revived the old boat "garage." New windows, cedar-shingle siding, flooring, and partitions for dressing rooms, a kitchen, bar, and bath turned the boat storage house into a wonderful poolhouse. Solar panels installed on the south-facing roof supplement an auxiliary heater and help reduce heating costs.

The architects' ingenious plan for the gently sloped site creates a raised pool terrace (right) that does not intrude on the flat landscape or block any vistas. The terrace is about two feet above the lower lawn level and two feet below the upper lawn level. The 4-foot-high hedge planted on the lower level thus appears as only two feet high on the pool level. The 5-foot-high hedge on the far side borders the neighbor's property. With new windows, French doors, and a refurbished interior, the old boat storage structure (above) makes a convenient pool house and a charming architectural accent. Just beyond the new pool house on the water, an existing building still functions as a boat garage. It also provides a picturesque backdrop and some shade for the only sitting area by the river. White trim contrasts sharply with the weathered cedar siding, decking, and chairs, all of which are well-suited to the natural, unadorned setting.

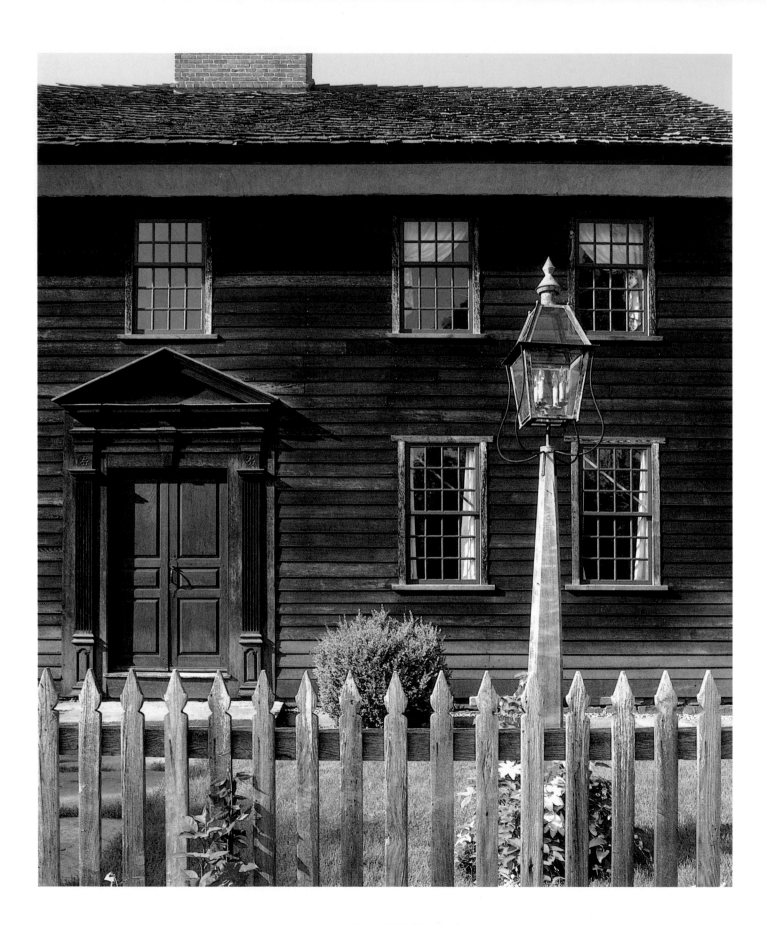

RESTORATION

FOR TODAY

I f the original occupants of this eighteenth-century house could see it now, they would certainly appreciate what the present owners have done to honor its heritage. Because the husband restores houses professionally, it was natural that his deep interest in and love for period architecture would carry over into the choice of a home for his own family.

The couple's overall planning began more than fifteen years ago with a quest for the right piece of land. They wanted an approach from the north, a sunset view, and an expansive southern exposure for all their outdoor activities. Once they succeeded in locating their nine-and-a-half-acre site, the search was on for an old house that they could move onto the property. What they found far exceeded their expectations: a well-documented structure built around 1720, with a central brick chimney, five-over-four fenestration, and an unusual framed plaster roof overhang. However, time had taken its toll on the exterior, and by 1820 it had acquired corner boards, new siding, and several coats of red paint. Since the interior was well-preserved, and the exterior would be a pleasure to restore, the ecstatic couple knew this was the house for them.

Before the house could be dismantled and reassembled on its new site, the land had to be cleared. Since the 30-by-40-foot structure was not to be simply a country cottage nestled in the woods, several acres of trees were removed to open up a space large enough to accommodate not only the house but a new porch and a swimming pool. The remaining woods became a privacy screen.

The new porch and pool area blend in beautifully with the restored house. The land slopes, so the front of the porch is at grade level, but the back required cutting and filling to build a stone

The classic facade of the restored house (opposite) faces the world much as it did back in the early eighteenth century. The weathered copper replica of a nineteenth-century lantern sits atop a chestnut post. A unifying design detail, chestnut also frames the windows and lends a traditional flavor to the picket fence. Large slabs of granite serve as the walkway to the authentically ornamented doorway.

A nineteenth-century goat cart filled with pots of bright red geraniums (above) adds a decorative, colorful accent in one corner of the pool terrace.

Impatiens and other annuals brighten the stone walkway to the porch (top). Fragrant wisteria softens the rugged architecture of an old wood shed add-on (above).

The porch addition (right) has a rustic character that is in complete harmony with the original part of the house. Old barn beams, a painted tin chandelier, stone flooring, and uphol-stered wicker furniture reinforce the feeling of an outdoor room with wide "windows" that look out over the pool and landscape beyond. Shadblow trees create shimmering patterns on the water's dark surface. Granite rectangles that rim the cleared area make picturesque seating.

basement foundation, an 8-foot-deep landing, a stone retaining wall, and 4-foot-wide stone steps that lead to the pool terrace. The porch, planned for comfortable outdoor living, has a rustic oak framework that came from old barns in the area and stone flooring that was set in mortar because of the basement below. The joints of the mortared foundation walls were deeply recessed to make them appear dry-set like the retaining wall.

The stonework adds immensely to the rugged appeal of the landscaping. The granite boulders and flat pavers in compatible colors were handpicked by the owner, who visualized where they would go while walking around quarries in Connecticut and Vermont: granite for foundation, retaining wall, and pool sur-rounds; pavers for porch and pool terrace.

The natural shape of the boulders dictated the free-form shape of the pool. Basically 16 by 34 feet in size, it was built of Gunite with swim-out steps, a layered waterfall, and a 42-inch-deep spa in one corner. A black plaster finish reflects surrounding shadblow trees and reinforces the pondlike look. The stone coping was mortared, but the terrace was dry-set in stone dust. Chosen for its clean, efficient heat and quick recovery, a gas-fired pool heater extends the swimming season.

Lighting plays a significant role in bringing the outdoors to life at night. The landscaping included the installation of a decorative copper post light to enhance the front entrance and a nine-arm chandelier made of tin to dress up the porch. Unobtrusive, func-tional lighting includes in-ground fixtures along the stone path by the pool, standard pool lights installed in a north wall so they would not be visible from the porch above, and low-wattage floodlights in the retaining wall, which cast a soft glow over the terrace.

The owners worked along with the construction crews, and it is no wonder, given their personal involvement, that the revitalized house and relandscaped grounds are central to their lives. In the summer, together with their four children, they spend a great deal of time outdoors, relaxing and entertaining on the porch and in or by the pool. And, as with most people who have a passion for restoration, they continue to formulate construction plans for the future. A guest house, barns, and garage are on the drawing boards.

With its cascading waterfall, dark reflective surface, and stone surround,
the swimming pool (opposite) cap-
tures the mood of a peaceful, sylvan
setting. Three majestic maple trees
(above) supply welcome shade and
changing shadow patterns. The
retaining wall makes a handsome
backdrop for poolside lounging and
for the mountain laurel's deep pink
blooms. The basement foundation for
the new porch provides abundant
storage plus bath and dressing room

facilities for the pool. The granite of
the pool terrace is continued in the
steps (right), which make getting in
and out of the water easy work. And
if sitting in the chairs is too hot,
lounging on the steps is a cool
alternative.

THE

PRACTICALITIES

PLANNING YOUR YARD

Designing or redesigning your yard requires careful and thorough planning. Unlike a "beautification" program which may result in little more than additional flowers or shrubs planted in existing beds, the goal in planning a yard is to unite house, gardens, walks, pool, and other landscape elements into a harmonious whole. The planning process will therefore take you to parts of your property that you may have ignored, force you to look at your land in new ways, and open up improvement possibilities that you may not have considered before.

To get started, ask yourself some specific questions. What do you like most about your site? What don't you like? Do you need screening for privacy, or do you want to take down some trees to let in more light and create more open space? Could you use a deck or patio for relaxing and entertaining outdoors? Do you want to include a swimming pool, a hot tub, or a tennis court?

DRAWING A PLAN

Whatever you decide, putting your ideas on paper is an important first step in designing your yard. Go outside and make a rough sketch showing the size and shape of your plot with your house positioned on it. If the builder, architect, a former owner, or the local buildings department can supply a plot plan, you can simply copy the basic dimensions for your sketch. However, you will still need to work on graph paper, preferably with quarter-inch squares, each to equal one foot, which is an easy-to-work-with gauge. Also, you will need a fifty- to one-hundred-foot tape, an architect's rule for reading dimensions in different scales, and a circle template or compass, which will enable you to depict the mature spreads of trees and shrubs with ease.

If you are sketching your plan from scratch, an easy way to measure your property is to choose a "baseline," a particular line from which all measurements will be made. One side of the house can serve this purpose, as can a straight row of stakes and cord placed along the length of the site. With luck, the grounds will have corner markers to simplify the process of getting boundary measurements.

Next, you should add to your sketch all the significant elements in your yard, including walks, driveway, fences, trees, shrubs, utility lines, old and new water pipes, downspouts, spigots, electrical outlets, and any ground-level changes that might require steps or a retaining wall. Even shadow patterns from trees and shrubs—yours and your neighbors'—are important factors in your plan, since they can determine the placement of ground covers and furnishings, for example. Clearly mark the side of your property that faces north to ensure that you always orient your plan correctly, and the scale to which the plan is drawn. Seasonal angles of the sun and the direction of prevailing winds in summer and winter are other pieces of information that belong on your base plan. Finally, when your rough sketch is complete, you should make a clean copy by transferring all the data more accurately and neatly to another piece of graph paper.

While you are analyzing your property and recording its vital statistics, be aware of other factors that may influence your design: views that you want to screen or retain; trees and shrubs that could be pruned or removed to let in more light; the microclimates which could affect the positioning of a vegetable garden or patio. Some spots may be too sunny, shady, or windy; others might present drainage problems, with rain and snow causing runoff that erodes some places and creates puddles in others. Bear in mind that landscaping can be designed to improve the energy efficiency of your home. Trees, shrubs, embankments, and water can all help to keep your house cool in summer. Large trees provide cooling shade, for example, and a small reflecting pool between south breezes and your house creates natural air-conditioning. A thick screen of vegetation both serves as a windbreak and absorbs noise; an embankment deflects the wind, in addition to providing privacy from the street. Furthermore, alterations to your house, such as the installation of a bay window or French doors, will create a closer indoor-outdoor relationship.

When planning different areas in your redesigned yard consider how they will be linked and integrated into the overall design. In this yard, garden designer Lisa Stamm smoothed the transition between the upper-deck level of the house and the pool with a gently sloping rock garden.

Where a house has a distinctive character, the design of the yard should enhance it, not compete with or overwhelm it. In this seventeenth-century restoration, the front yard was deliberately kept simple and devoid of large or showy plantings, for example, which keeps it true to the style of the period and in harmony with the facade. A plain picket fence creates a neat front yard, and large rough flagstones delineate the path to the front door, retaining the classical symmetry of the exterior. No foundation plantings obscure the lines of the house.

With tracing paper overlaid on your base plan, experiment with different layouts until you determine what works well—and what suits your site. Think of your landscape as a room: paving, lawn, and ground covers are the floor; fences, hedges, and screens are the walls; trees, arbors, and the sky are the ceiling; plantings, seating, and lighting are the furnishings. When placing the new elements you would like to include, take into account existing obstructions such as water pipes or utility lines, as well as assets such as a handsome view or a well-placed patio. Design principles apply to the outdoors as much as they do to the indoors: Scale, line, pattern, shape, and texture, for instance, are all important. Your yard will derive its individual character from the lines and patterns that are formed by such landscape elements as a deck, pool, fence, trees, an arbor, and planting beds.

Since integrating the new landscape plan with the house is an objective, you should choose complementary design elements and materials to ensure a sense of continuity and cohesion. For example, a house with a rustic, country flavor calls for an informal landscape with cottage-type gardens. On the other hand, traditional French or English architectural styles are often enhanced by formal beds and an ordered, symmetrical plan. Sometimes rules of thumb can be broken—or bent—with fine results, but generally speaking, house and landscape should blend harmoniously in scale and mood.

Before you turn your drawing into reality, prepare a mock-up in the yard so that you can correct what you don't like. Stakes and string let you visualize straight lines; a garden hose or rope will delineate curves for walks and planting beds. Make adjustments as you go, checking for wind, sun, shade, noise, views, and privacy. Look at the overall pattern you have made from an upstairs window or elevated ground.

What makes landscaping so difficult—and fascinating—is that you have to visualize how plants will look in two, six, and even ten years, when they have matured. So, when placing trees and shrubs on your plan, make sure you allow for and indicate their mature dimensions, which are normally given when the tree is purchased.

General Yard-Planning Tips

1. If you are landscaping in stages, plant trees and major shrubs first. Evergreens planted on the north side of your house will act as buffers to cold winter winds. Deciduous trees on the south side of the house will supply shade by blocking the sunlight in summer and allowing warming sunlight to reach the house during the cold winter months.

2. When planning walkways, 4 or 5 feet is wide enough for 2 people, particularly at an entry, where you want to express a feeling of welcome. If walkways intersect, people cut across corners and trample grass or other plantings; round intersections for a smoother turn.

3. In designing steps, the relationship between treads and risers is important. Generally, twice the riser plus the depth of the tread should equal 25 to 27 inches. A 6-inch-high riser and a 15-inch-deep tread is a comfortable step. For a ramp-type stairway, you might have a 4-inch-high riser with a 19-inch (or even deeper) tread.

4. Do not plant trees or shrubs where they will obstruct visibility at the entrance to the driveway.

5. A 4-foot wide gate allows a wheelbarrow to pass through.

6. Position seating areas in the yard where they can take advantage of pleasing views.

7. Design a patio or deck with proportions related to its use. If it is too large, it will lack a sense of enclosure and require several seating areas.

8. Place plant containers and furniture on a deck or patio as you would furniture in a room.

9. To create more interest and greater impact, plant shrubs and flowers in masses of three, five, seven, or more, depending on the available space.

10. Site a swimming pool so that it is sheltered from prevailing winds and is warmed by afternoon sunlight.

11. Site flower beds and ornamental trees and shrubs where they can be enjoyed from the main rooms of the house.

12. Always design a property keeping in mind the time required for its maintenance.

FENCES AND WALLS

Fences and walls are decorative and multi-functional elements of the yard. For those living in close proximity to neighbors, they provide privacy and delineate boundaries without being unfriendly barriers. If you live on or near a busy street, they can effectively muffle the noise of passing cars and trucks. (The right design can buffer wind as well.) And fences and walls are a practical way to keep children and pets within safe bounds. Moreover, in addition to their many practical functions, fences and walls serve an aesthetic purpose, forming "outdoor rooms" of different character and creating or reinforcing a specific mood. A picket fence, for example, gives a house a friendly, welcoming air, whereas a brick wall presents a formal and, if high enough, forbidding face to neighbors and passersby.

If you plan to build a fence or wall in your yard, consider the kind of look you want and what you want to say about your household, as well as your practical needs. Most fences are built from wood or metal, and walls from stone, brick, or concrete block. Although only man-made boundaries will be discussed here, also keep in mind hedges of trees or shrubs, which are an appealing natural boundary to a garden. These living walls do, however, take time to mature—even the fastest growing evergreen will increase its height by at most six to seven inches a year—and they must be pruned and sheared annually to stay in a desired shape.

For perimeter walls or fences, it is important to verify your property lines before work is begun. Exact boundaries can be

Mixing materials can give added interest and character to a fence or wall. Here the undulating lines of a simple wooden fence, painted white, set atop a dry-set retaining wall, soften a boundary (top).

A dry-set wall of rough-hewn granite, (above) designed by Randolph Marshall, makes a suitable boundary marker in a rustic setting. In a suburban or urban setting, however, a solid wall of this height might look forbidding.

difficult to determine. If no record is available on file or in the deed to the property, you can have the site resurveyed by a civil engineer or surveyor.

You will also need to consult a local building inspector before planning a wall or fence. Almost every area has its own zoning laws that limit the height to which a fence or wall can be built. Exact regulations vary, but three and a half feet for front fences and six feet for back fences are the maximum allowable heights in many regions. Local laws may also require fencing of a minimum height around swimming pools, spas, and hot tubs. These regulations can be quite specific, but they are a prudent protection for children, pets, and nonswimmers.

FENCES

Generally, fences are less expensive, easier to install, and more versatile than masonry walls. Moreover, they come in a variety of styles, ranging from functional chain link to ornamental iron to textured wood in open or solid designs.

The style, material, finish, and scale of a fence should all be compatible with your house and yard, even if it is to serve merely as a support and backdrop for plantings or as a boundary marker. If the exterior of your house is clapboard or wood shingles, for example, you might erect a fence of the same material and finish. Also, interesting effects can be achieved by combining styles. Scalloped boards look lovely with spade-capped posts; an airy latticework top lightens and adds a charming decorative fillip to solid boards.

Don't settle for stockade fences simply because they are economical and easy to install. Make sure that your fence meets your aesthetic needs—and your neighbors'—as well. A one-sided fence might look good in your yard but offend your neighbors. A solid fence that you can't see over can feel claustrophobic, especially if the property is small.

A sturdy chain-link or wire-mesh fence is often a good choice to surround a tennis court or pool, or to protect children and pets. While they offer good security, these fences are plainly not the solution if you seek privacy, however. But chain link and wire mesh are long lasting and economical materials. And because fencing is made by the roll it is quick to install. These straightforward fences are also easy to maintain and need no finish. Perhaps the major disadvantage of such fences is their frankly utilitarian appearance. Yet, kept dark in color, they will recede into the background. And with such evergreen vines as English ivy (*Hedera helix*) or big-leaf wintercreeper (*Euonymus fortunei*) trained up their sides, the industrial look of these fences will virtually disappear over time.

An iron fence is a more formal, decorative solution than chain link or wire mesh, and perhaps most suitable to an urban environment. Many of today's reproductions of the old handcrafted wrought-iron fences are precast of tubular steel, some with the curlicues that frame gingerbread Victorian houses so well, others with neoclassical motifs more suitable to Colonial or Federal period houses, and still others that complement contemporary architectural themes. Like wire-mesh and chain-link fences, an iron fence is not for anyone who needs complete privacy or insulation from the elements. But if the fence is high enough, it does afford a good measure of security. The design and construction of an iron fence are best left to a professional, making it an expensive choice. Maintenance, however, is relatively easy: A simple coat of paint is the best finish for an iron fence.

Since wooden fences come in seemingly innumerable styles and can suit almost any purpose, wood is perhaps the material that first comes to mind when thinking about boundaries. There are styles that allow light and air in and yet afford privacy, that mark boundaries while maintaining a sense of openness, that admit light while still effectively buffering winds.

Ready-made wooden fencing usually comes in six- or eight-foot sections that are four, six, or eight feet high. The posts, which should be set in gravel or concrete one foot below the depth to which the frost penetrates (the average depth of frost penetration is one to two feet), are usually four or six inches square. Your choice of gravel or concrete will depend on the load the footing has to bear and the stability of your soil.

The heartwood of redwood, cedar, and cypress is ideal for wooden fencing since it is naturally resistant to decay and insect damage. Although expensive, these woods are also popular because of their texture, grain, and the color they acquire when left to weather. An economical and equally dependable option is lumber that has been pressure treated with chemicals that prevent deterioration.

The split-rail fence, which easily follows the contours of a landscape, has a rustic quality that is perhaps most appropriate to a rural or semirural setting. While effectively delineating the boundaries of your property, it also offers continuous views inside and out, uniting your yard with the landscape beyond. (It is not, therefore, the fence for security or privacy.) Climbing plants such as roses or wisteria will enhance the fence's natural unity with its surroundings. A split-rail design is of moderate cost, does not take very long to build, and, because it is not solid, is relatively easily installed on an undulating site.

Wooden Fence Styles

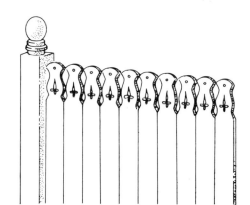
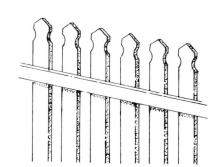
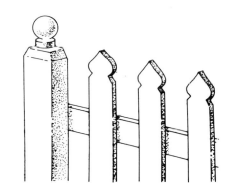

Variations in picket-fence patterns make this one of the most versatile of fence styles.

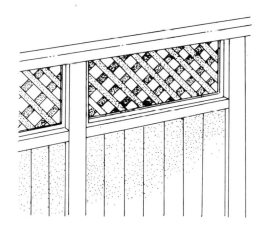
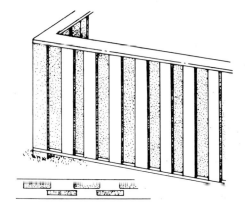
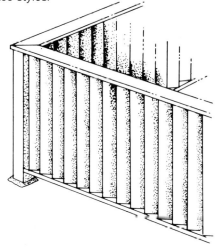

Lattice lightens a simple board fence.

Board-on-board fencing offers both privacy and ventilation.

A louvered fence is good if you need privacy and security, but do not want to feel closed in.

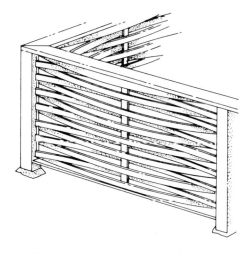
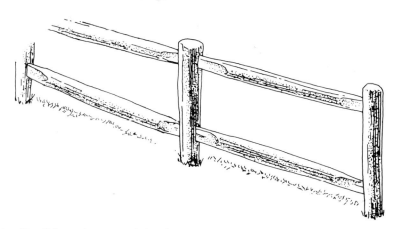

A basket-weave fence gives the yard a friendly, rustic look.

A charming split-rail fence is appropriate where privacy is not a requirement.

Setting Fence Posts

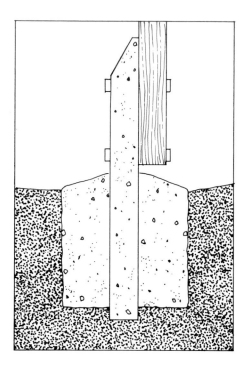 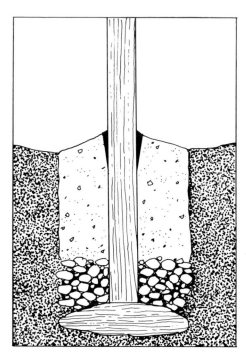

Over time, wooden fences will rot and weaken, although setting wooden posts in concrete will delay this. Bolting the posts to a concrete spur set in a concrete base, far left, so that the wood is not in contact with the ground and can dry more quickly, will delay rotting still further.

Alternatively, near left, set a large stone at the bottom of each post hole to protect the end of the post from sitting in water. Keeping the post vertical, backfill with rubble for about 4 inches before pouring concrete around the post. To prevent the concrete from cracking in freezing weather, create expansion collars: Cut two wooden wedges to the width of the post. Oil these wedges and insert them on either side of the post before you pour in the concrete. When the concrete is dry, remove the wedges and fill the spaces with tar or sand.

The unpretentious basket-weave fence has a charming rustic look about it. It offers good security and a great deal of privacy without imparting an unfriendly air. A basket-weave fence also softens the effects of wind and sun and blocks noise. If you want to minimize the undulation of the boards and give the fence a more graceful look, run a thin spacer down the center of each bay. A basket-weave fence, which requires moderate construction time, may be stained or left to weather naturally.

A picket fence may well be the most popular—and versatile—fence style. Appropriate in rural, suburban, or city settings, the bright white of a classic picket fence makes an especially charming surround for cottage gardens and colonial-style houses. There are also variations in picket patterns to give you almost any look you want, be it formal, welcoming, or rural. Although this is not the fence for privacy, it is a good choice to protect children or pets without making them feel confined. A picket fence will also block drifting snow and, if the pickets are spaced closely enough together, soften breezes.

It can be difficult today to find some of the fancy tops and finials seen in the picket fences of the past. Lumberyards carry limited pre-cut shapes, and to cut your own special shapes is time-consuming, as so many pickets are needed for a fence. While the cost of materials is relatively low, construction time for a long picket fence is relatively high.

An attractive choice for today's suburban settings is the louvered fence, which simultaneously offers ventilation, security, and privacy. It also filters sunlight and softens wind, making it a good choice for a patio. A louvered fence may be painted, stained, or allowed to weather naturally. Since the boards of a louvered fence are angled, a great number of them are required, making this a more expensive fence that takes longer to construct from scratch than other board fencing.

Board-on-board fencing can combine excellent privacy (if it is six or eight feet high) with ventilation in city lots. Because the boards are fastened to a central nailer, alternating sides board by board, the fence is identical on both sides, eliminating an unsightly view on your neighbors' side. Plantings of shrubs, taller flowers, or ornamental grasses will soften the look of the board-on-board fence and give it grace and character. This fence is relatively modest in cost, but it can be time-consuming to construct.

The regularity of this fence's lattice grid is a perfect foil for the lively profusion of colors and textures in the flowers and foliage in front of it, some of which have begun climbing the fence.

An entrance sets the tone for a property. Here, the appeal of an elegant gate with fine details is enhanced by a bed of red and pink astilbe and purple and white irises.

WALLS

Although more expensive and more difficult to erect than fences, masonry walls do create a more permanent and architecturally substantial boundary. A stone wall can look as if it had been there for generations; brick, another ancient material, can also look timeless, and it ages nicely; the first impression of concrete block is one of lasting strength and sturdiness. These solid materials all present a strong visual barrier, whether used at the perimeter of a property or to separate or unite different sections within a yard. A wall can make a patio either stand apart from or blend harmoniously with the rest of the yard, for example. Also, masonry makes a better sound barrier than a fence for those who live on heavily traveled roads, near a highway, or in other areas with significant noise levels.

Masonry walls generally require concrete footings poured beneath the frost line. Without a proper foundation, a mortar wall can shift and crack. However, no foundation is likely to be needed to provide support for low, raised beds, walls less than twelve inches high, or curved walls.

As with fences, your wall should be of a piece with your house, yard, and the area you live in. If you live in a part of the country in which fieldstone is abundant, a wall of the same material would probably be suitable, for example. A brick house should have a brick wall designed to suit the architectural style of the house, whether it be contemporary, Colonial, or otherwise.

The rustic stone wall is perhaps the archetypal boundary marker. Stone's natural affinity with the landscape makes it a popular material for wall construction. Dry-set fieldstone is an appropriate marker for the edges of a rugged country property. It has the added charm of being reminiscent of this nation's early settlers.

Concrete Block

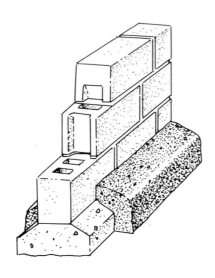

To build a simple wall of concrete, you will need three basic types of block: capping block for the top, stretcher block for the middle, and corner block for the ends of the wall. Other types are available for design variations.

Stone walls can be dry set or you can use mortar. A dry-set wall plays up the character of each stone and has crevices that you can fill with soil and such hardy rock plants as sedum and phlox. One advantage of a mortared wall ("wet wall") is that it requires fewer stones. Without mortar, you must be certain that the vertical joints are not continuous, and you must stabilize the wall at regular intervals with stones laid perpendicular to the direction of the wall. Fieldstone, which is uncut and irregular in shape and weight, is more difficult to work with than cut stone or concrete block or brick. And it is costly, unless you already have a sufficient supply on your property to excavate and reposition.

The beauty, versatility, and durability of brick have made it a long-standing garden favorite. Suitable for a house of almost any style, brick comes in enough different colors and textures to present almost unlimited design possibilities. It can be laid on end, set on edge, angled to produce graceful curves, and stacked with open spaces to create a screen. As a bonus, brick develops a lovely patina with time. However, since it is more expensive to build a high wall of brick than of concrete block, brick is often the choice for smaller areas such as planting beds, gates, posts and the supports for panels of iron, lattice, or wood. Low brick walls can become decorative borders at streetside; within your garden they can double as seating and planting boxes.

Because of their small size—a standard brick is $2\frac{1}{4} \times 3\frac{1}{4} \times 8$ inches—it takes longer to construct a brick wall than one of concrete block. Nevertheless, bricks are easy to handle and position, and their uniform shape makes them easier to work with than stone. Walls over two feet high need to be laid in a double thickness of interlocking patterns. The bricks that are laid horizontally, following the line of the wall, are called "stretchers." Those laid on end, perpendicular to the direction of the wall, are called "headers." The specific arrangement of headers and stretchers within a wall is called the "bond." While the advantages of one bond over another are primarily aesthetic, there are slight differences in strength, so your choice of bond may depend on the thickness and height of the wall: If your wall is one brick thick, for example, your bond may comprise only stretchers. Regardless of the bond used, a brick wall must also be "capped" to protect it from the elements, since most brick is weatherproof on one face only. A row of bricks set on edge serves, as does a concrete slab.

Concrete block can provide complete privacy and security. It looks best in an urban environment. It is the most economical material to use for a wall and is virtually unsurpassable for strength, but unfinished it is also the most uninteresting. However, concrete block can be covered with two coats of stucco, the last colored to match your house, or it can be embellished or camouflaged with vines or climbing roses. Concrete block comes in a variety of finishes, from coarse to smooth to glazed.

Building with concrete block is easier and cheaper than with brick or stone, for the blocks are larger—a standard size is $7\frac{5}{8} \times 7\frac{5}{8} \times 15\frac{5}{8}$ inches—and walls go up fast. There are three basic types of concrete block used in a wall. The "stretcher" block, which is perforated three times from top to bottom and is convex at the ends, is used to form the bulk of the wall; the "solid-top"—or capping—block comprises the top row of blocks on the wall, and the "corner" block, with one flat end, is used at the edges of the wall.(Ask your supplier about other types that are available to suit your specific needs.) A wall of concrete block needs a protective capping, in addition to the capping block; paving slabs and wood that have been sloped to allow for runoff of rainwater usually work well.

Both brick and concrete block can be erected as openwork screens that offer views, breezes, and a play of light and shadow. Available in a variety of designs, screen blocks can be used either alone or with solid units to form decorative geometric patterns that allow air to circulate. However, openwork brick or concrete screens are not load bearing.

Erecting a fence or wall on your property involves forethought and work. Yet, if you are more sensitive to the practical and aesthetic requirements of your property, the fence or wall will be an integral part of the pleasure you derive from your yard.

Hedges

Hedges are living fences that, depending on the shrub chosen, can serve many of the same purposes as a wooden fence or brick wall—as windbreak, boundary marker, or screen—while also blending easily into the surrounding landscape. A hedge of shrubs or small trees can add color, textures, and even scent to the yard although unlike fences or walls, of course, they require some time to mature and will need annual maintenance.

Generally, this maintenance consists of pruning or clipping. Deciduous hedges should be cut in spring, midsummer, and early fall (but no later than early September) as necessary to keep them in shape. Evergreen hedges should be trimmed just after the new growth is made in spring, in late May or early June. Keep the shape of the hedge wider at the bottom than the top so that light still reaches the lower branches.

The most popular hedge choices include privet (*Ligustrum*) and two evergreens, boxwood (*Buxus*) and yew (*Taxus*), all of which take well to trimming and shaping by virtue of their small leaves and compact growth. Evergreens such as arborvitae (*Thuja*) and hemlock (*Tsuga*) are relatively easy to establish and will quickly form a dense screen. Hollies (*Ilex*) and some barberies (*Berberis*) also make excellent hedges. But if you can use something less formal, the choice becomes much wider and embraces many varieties of the flowering shrubs used in the garden, including rhododendron and azalea, spirea, viburnum, forsythia, and shrub roses.

RETAINING WALLS

Land that has significant slopes and hills may have to be reshaped to be made more usable. The leveled slopes and graded sites of a reshaped plot are created by retaining walls. A retaining wall, which is simply a barrier that holds earth in place, can also discourage erosion and ease the transition from one level of your yard to another. A series of low walls will terrace a hill into manageable increments. And since trees do not fare well if their roots and immediate surroundings are disturbed, retaining walls can save the life of a prized specimen that has been stranded by the regrading of a site. If the grade has been lowered, a raised bed, kept in place by a retaining wall, will keep the soil at its original level. If the ground has been raised, a well built around the tree and the newly raised soil, retained with a wall, will protect the tree's roots.

Although essentially functional, retaining walls also have an aesthetic value in the landscape. If a slope is gentle, a two-foot-high retaining wall can be used to enclose a patio and at the same time double as garden seating. Low walls that retain soil for raised planting beds add a pleasing change of elevation in the landscape. Indeed, a raised flower or vegetable garden one or two-feet high is easier to tend than one at ground level and as a freestanding, three- or four-sided structure, it will be a focal point of a yard. Simple steps can also act as retaining walls that connect one part of a yard with another. If a slope is long and steep, a series of low walls alternating with steps is more

pleasing to the eye than a single high wall. In addition, such wall/step combinations create terraced areas that can easily be landscaped. Containing a whole hillside of soil, however, may involve building a high, solid wall with a sturdy foundation.

Since a wall that is three feet high or less does not need a foundation, if you are handy you can probably build one yourself. However, any wall over three feet high requires an engineer's expertise in designing drainage solutions and in reinforcing techniques, and specifying foundation depths.

Drainage is a critical concern in the construction of retaining walls. Heavy rains and melting snow saturate the earth, and in their downhill flow they can exert enough

Within a property, a retaining wall can create a level, well-defined area for recreation, relaxation, or for a planting bed. The dense ground cover of periwinkle planted at the base of this wall both softens the stone wall and solves the problem of mowing this difficult area.

pressure on a wall to demolish it. If the water is allowed to run off through "weep holes," either gaps in the jointing or hollow pipes set through the wall at regular intervals, then the water pressure on the wall is reduced. Adding an infill of gravel behind the wall further alleviates the pressure and directs the water to the drainage holes. A drainpipe installed at the base of the gravel, parallel to the wall, will also help get rid of excess water, and a gutter at the top will carry off surface floods. If this water cannot go into a sewer system, it may have to be diverted to a drainage ditch.

When deciding whether to build a retaining wall of concrete, stone, brick, or wood, consider how the wall will be used, how strong it will have to be (that is, how much earth it will have to hold back), and how it will blend with your yard.

MATERIALS

Concrete poured in forms on the site offers great strength for holding back the earth. Hollow concrete blocks, reinforced with steel rods, filled with grout, and mortared into a concrete foundation, also make stable retaining walls. Bricks, because of their small size and the need for many mortar joints, are not practical for high retaining walls, but they are sturdy and beautiful at or under three feet. Retaining walls made of concrete block and brick, in particular, may need capping to prevent water from seeping into cracks, freezing, and causing damage to the joints. Flat paving stones are often used for this purpose.

Natural stone, dry-set or mortared, creates handsome, strong retaining walls, particularly if angled, or built on a batter, into the earth. If dry-set, the stones should be tilted two to three inches for every foot; if mortared, one to two inches per foot. Cut-stone walls give a more formal, architectural appearance than uncut fieldstone. A low, dry-set fieldstone wall needs no foundation, and it will be self-draining because the irregular shapes of the stones leave gaps in the wall. These gaps can be filled with soil to provide spots for plants, the roots of which will also help retain the soil.

A masonry retaining wall that is higher than four feet will need a strong concrete foundation or footings built below the frost line in freezing climates.

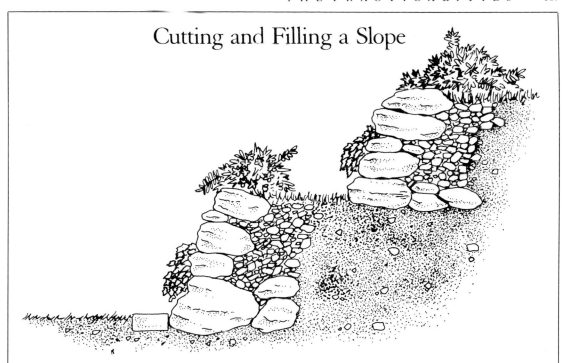

Cutting and Filling a Slope

If a slope is no more than 2 or 3 feet high, you can regrade it with a series of small retaining walls. Very simply, this entails moving the soil to create a series of small terraces—each held in place with a retaining wall—suitable for planting a ground cover such as ivy or periwinkle and rock plants or prostrate shrubs such as creeping juniper or cotoneaster. The roots will help hold the soil, and the foliage will soften the wall as it spills over the edge. Stones, landscape timbers, and boards set on edge are all suitable materials for the walls.

Wood is not as permanent as masonry, but pressure-treated planks, landscape timbers, and railroad ties, properly anchored, offer an inexpensive, rustic look for steps, low walls, and raised beds. Available in four-by-four inch and six-by-six inch sizes that are six or eight feet long, they are readily available at lumberyards and garden centers.

PLANTINGS

Hardy, easy-care plantings add the finishing touch to a retaining wall and soften the rigidity of its structure. They should be in a scale that suits the setting and be placed in the soil while it is still loose and workable. Compact succulents, such as sedums and hen-and-chicks, will nestle gracefully into the crevices of rocks. Flowering perennials such as dianthus, basket-of-gold, candy tuft, moss pink phlox, campanula, and aubrieta have colorful blooms that will spill over a retaining wall in beguiling ways. The subtle textures, shapes, and hues of low-growing artemisia, blue fescue, heather, and dwarf species of creeping evergreens are also appropriate plants for a wall.

Because the construction of retaining walls can be complex, you may need professional help. If your slope is steep, soil type is a problem, reinforcements are troublesome, foundations are difficult, or your land is in an earthquake zone, consult with a structural engineer, licensed builder, or masonry contractor, as your needs dictate. Also, your local building codes may well require a permit, professional supervision, and inspection by a local official.

DRIVEWAYS

Homeowners too often ignore driveways and parking areas when planning their landscaping projects, but in today's automobile-oriented society, they certainly deserve as much attention as any other yard detail. Like the one-horse shay, the one-car family has almost disappeared. Moreover, four-wheel-drive vehicles, vans, and pick-up trucks are part of many people's lives, and all these larger vehicles must be accommodated.

Driveways and parking areas, as the initial contact with many homes, should be easy to see and maneuver. You may therefore want to remove trees or shrubs that obstruct the line of sight from the road. On the other hand, you may want to put in plantings that outline the driveway, define a parking bay, mask views of the garage, or soften the look of the paving. Just make sure you maintain a pleasing balance between paving and plantings.

In combination with an entrance courtyard or a back parking area, a smooth, hard-surfaced driveway can double as a space for basketball games, tricycle riding,

A driveway need not be a neutral element in yard design. Here, KenMark Landscaping mixed materials—asphalt and Belgian blocks—to add character and visual interest to the drive so that it plays a major role in the property's entrance. The large Katsura tree in the center not only defines the turnaround and brick parking area, but adds an elegant note that completes the design.

and other recreational activities. A parking area adjacent to the kitchen or service area facilitates the carrying of groceries and other packages that go in or out of your house regularly. When placed near the main entrance, the parking area is a welcome mat for friends.

When planning the driveway's layout, make sure it is in harmony with your land and house. It should neither be boring nor overwhelm your property. For example, instead of connecting the street to the front or rear entry with a straight line, consider using a curve if there is space. It will cost more, but the change of views will create more visual interest. From a practical standpoint, a winding drive can lessen the steepness of a slope. Make sure, though, to avoid any tight curves that could become dangerous on ice or snow. Also, do not mix straight stretches with a series of curves, as this will disrupt the smooth flow.

Drives should never be less than ten feet wide; twelve feet is better. If curves are sharp, allow twelve to fourteen feet. The width of a curve depends on the turning space a car needs and should be at least one-third wider than the car. The grade of your drive should not exceed 1¾ inches per running foot or vehicles will scrape the street when going in and out.

Proper drainage is an important consideration when planning a driveway and parking area. If not built for water runoff, they can become big puddles in heavy rains or ice slicks in freezing weather. A gravel surface could be washed away. Allow a slope away from your house or garage of about a quarter inch per foot. A one-inch center crown will allow the water to run off both sides, either into the ground or into cobbled or graveled gutters.

The form that a driveway and parking area takes will also be influenced by the size and shape of your site. If space permits, a circular drive, which delivers you and your guests to your front door, offers a gracious and friendly greeting. This layout is also a great convenience, since it allows you to drive in and out with ease and provides extra space for parking. On a large plot, the drive can continue to a garage and service area at the rear. However, a circular plan is equally appropriate for a modest house. At an entry door, a twenty-two foot straight stretch will be needed to parallel park a car, and an extra width of at least nine feet can serve as an extra parking space or a bypass. A U-shaped drive that connects the street and front entry also allows cars to go in and out without having a back-up or turn-around space. At a side entrance, this plan can facilitate the loading and unloading of packages. Planting the center of the circle or U-shape with trees, shrubs, flowers, or a ground cover will integrate the drive with the rest of the landscape and visually break up the expanse of paving.

If space is limited and you live on a busy street, it is a good idea to add a turn-around space to avoid having to back out of the garage onto the street. For a two-car garage, which is usually twenty feet wide, the back-up space should be at least twelve feet wide. Obviously, the wider it is, the more room there will be to park and turn. Railroad ties or some other wheel stop (or "bumper strip") will keep cars off the lawn.

PARKING AREAS

Diagonal parking, with car stalls clearly delineated, makes efficient use of space. The parking area can be an extension of a turn-around near the garage, or it can provide off-street parking up front. You will need eighteen feet for the length of each car, nine feet for each width, and three feet for door

clearance between the cars. Railroad ties or concrete are practical as bumper strips for each stall. For three cars, this zig-zag arrangement requires a space fifty-six by twenty-two feet.

Another alternative is a parking bay. This can be adjacent to a turn-around and is convenient for larger vehicles. The bay can also be placed up front to give guests easy access to the house. However, cars have to back out into the street, which can be hazardous. Two cars need a space twenty-two feet long and wide, flared at the rear for backing out. A bumper strip of concrete or railroad ties can define the bay.

Parallel parking is an option where a space is too narrow for diagonal parking or a bay. For this plan, a section of the drive is widened—made to extend into the lawn. Allow a width of eight feet and length of twenty-two feet to parallel park each car. An edging of railroad ties or low shrubs will help define the parking area.

MATERIALS

Since the materials used for the driveway and parking area will affect the overall look of the yard, they should be compatible with the exterior of the house and with the surrounding landscape. Concrete, asphalt, and gravel are common driveway materials. More decorative materials such as cobblestones, bricks, landscape timbers, and pressure-treated wood are best used for finishing touches. They are all suitable durable edging for the curbs of paved drives and parking areas.

A concrete driveway will have to be at least four inches thick, and six to eight inches for heavy trucks. Although long-wearing and low maintenance, concrete can stain, and it can be glaring unless colored or embedded with pebble aggregate. The ad-

In this design by Glen Fries, Belgian block defines the sinuous curves of the driveway as curbing and also articulates the parking area at the front of the house.

dition of a pebble aggregate adds an earthy color and texture that enhance surrounding garden trees and shrubs.

Asphalt—or *blacktop*, as it is often called—is more economical than concrete. Although quite serviceable, asphalt can soften in the heat, and it needs sealing every couple of years. At least two inches of asphalt are required over a two-inch gravel base. If easy snow and ice removal is one of your dreams, consider burying heating cables in an asphalt pavement.

Gravel or crushed rock and such other loose-fill materials as rounded pebbles and river rock require less grading and subsurface preparation than concrete or asphalt. They are laid over a two-inch leveled sand base. Although not as long-lasting as hard-surface paving, loose fill materials are lower in cost. Also, they reinforce the rustic flavor of a country setting. One limitation of loose-fill materials is their tendency to spread, though steel edging will help keep them in place. In addition, they are not as inviting as paved surfaces for ballgames and bicycle riding. Available in colors, gravel is sometimes rolled into asphalt to relate the driveway surface to other garden details. Another advantage of gravel is that it can serve as a base for concrete or asphalt paving at some future time.

Although brick can be used to pave an entire driveway and parking area, it is costly and is more often used as part of the design. For example, brick inlaid in concrete can echo the pattern of a walk or entrance courtyard. If used for a driveway, brick should be mortared over a concrete base to take the weight of the cars.

Driveway Designs

Where there is space, a circular driveway with extra space for parking or passing in front of the house is both elegant and convenient for entering and exiting a property.

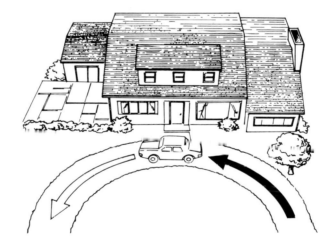

Like the circular plan, a U-shaped, or horseshoe, drive brings guests right to the front door. And again, there is no backing onto the street.

On smaller properties or where the house is at right angles to the street, a drive with a turnaround eliminates backing onto the street.

WALKWAYS AND STEPS

Walks and garden steps are the physical links among various parts of your yard. Walkways can link a part of the house to a functional area such as the sidewalk, garage, or parking area: With a firm, comfortable, slip-proof surface, they can safely and conveniently deliver guests and groceries to the house. They can, on the other hand, have the additional purpose of leading people *away* from the house, around the yard or garden, offering choice views of flowers, trees, and garden structures. When they perform the latter function, walkways do not take the most direct route from point A to point B, but meander a bit, perhaps moving you away from a not so desirable view, or pausing by a pleasant one, thus encouraging you to move at a leisurely pace.

DESIGN AND MATERIALS

Even a utilitarian walk, however, need not be completely prosaic. An entrance walk, for example, does not have to be a straight, narrow strip of concrete. In fact, since the entrance walk sets the tone of your property at the outset, it should be as welcoming as possible. If you already have a straight concrete walk, you might make it wider and more interesting with a border at the same

A walkway need not be the straightest route between two points. Adding curves will not only give it visual interest, but can improve the surrounding area as well. This curved brick walk blends into a welcoming patio with an interesting mix of brick and flagstones.

Even the most straightforward walkways and steps can be enriched by an interplay of textures and colors. In the flagstone walkway and steps here, the orchestration of earthy grays, along with the contrast of smooth and rough textures, adds subtle but nonetheless strong visual interest.

level on both sides. A frame of brick laid in sand, for example, could double the walk's size and add a decorative touch as well. Pressure-treated wood, landscape timbers, and stones are other materials that can be striking trim for walks.

A new walk should be four to five feet wide so that two people can travel side by side. Consider as well designing your entry with a curving brick or flagstone walk that culminates in a small courtyard by the front door. Gentle curves break up the rigidity and boredom of too many straight lines, and they are aesthetically more satisfying.

A garden walk, particularly one that meanders a bit, can be narrower than a more functional walk—it may be only 2½ or 3 feet wide if you want. However, you may want to make it wider in order to push a wheelbarrow or other equipment from one place to another.

Whereas a utilitarian walk should be of a hard, solid materials such as brick, concrete, or flagstone, the more rustic garden walk can be surfaced in a soft material such as sound-absorbing wood chips or crushed stones spread over a compacted base. Random stepping-stones of slate or fieldstone are another informal option. (For the placement of stepping-stones, note the pattern your footprints make and set the stones accordingly.) Such plantings as thyme, moss, and creeping mint are effective among the stones as long as they do not interfere with the paving itself. An informal walk or path should not have a strictly defined border, which lends a more formal air, but should spill over and into its surroundings.

While establishing both the major access routes to and from your house and the secondary routes around your yard, you need to consider drainage. If there are dips and low spots in your ground where water collects, you will need to either regrade, put in a gravel-filled ditch, or slope any paving slightly to allow surface water to run off. (Sloping the walkway prevents freezing water from heaving the soil and cracking the paving.)

STEPS

You may need not only walkways on your property, but garden steps to connect different levels of your yard. The design and materials used for the steps should harmonize with the walks and paths. Steps, which must be comfortable and stable underfoot,

Walkways

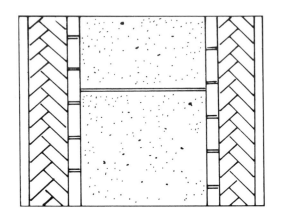

Concrete with herringbone brick border

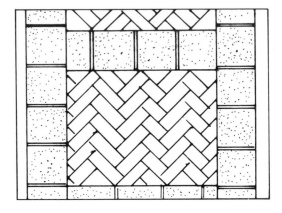

Herringbone brick with concrete slabs

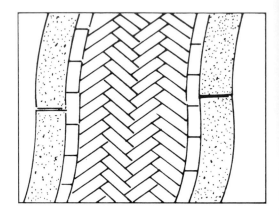

Serpentine brick with concrete border

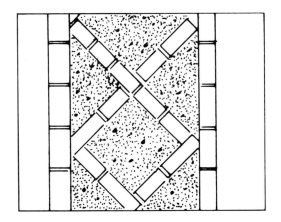

Brick and gravel

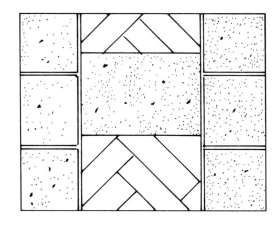

Bluestone and concrete pavers

Fieldstone set in grass

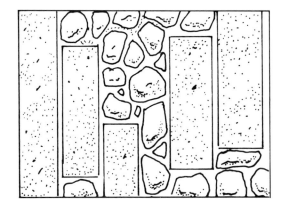

Bluestone and fieldstone

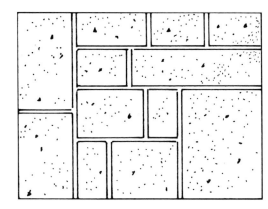

Bluestone in varying sizes

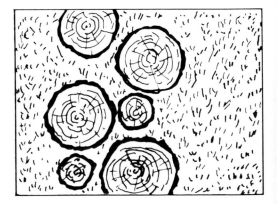

Wood rounds set in grass

Stone is here used in many forms—fine pea gravel for the stair treads and walkway and rough-cut stone for the dry-set retaining wall—to create a composition that is ordered yet fits in perfectly with its country setting.

can take many forms, from a large natural stone anchored in the ground to the more formal composition made with concrete poured into forms constructed of two by sixes, and finished with exposed aggregate or trimmed with brick or treated wood. Risers of railroad ties and treads of brick also make handsome steps.

Both risers and treads need a stable foundation. The ratio between riser and tread is critical: As a rule, twice the riser plus the depth of the tread should equal twenty five to twenty seven inches. For instance, a step with a six-inch riser and a fifteen-inch tread is comfortable to walk on, as is a four-inch riser and a nineteen-inch tread, which might be used for a series of steps on a gradual incline. Wide, deep steps are more inviting than narrow and steep ones. Also, steps should be evenly spaced so that people do not have to change their stride each time they move up or down.

The character of walkways and steps depends on the materials of which they are constructed. The way the materials are used also determines the final effect, be it rustic and casual or formal and elegant. Brick, concrete, flagstone, stones, tile, loose aggregates, and wood are all possible materials for walkways and steps, each suiting certain purposes and budgets better than others.

Brick is an old favorite, adding warmth, texture, and pattern to even the plainest yard. Its adaptability to different patterns also makes brick a flexible tool for visually uniting walks with patios. Widely available in a variety of types, sizes, and colors, brick

Laying a Brick Walk in Sand

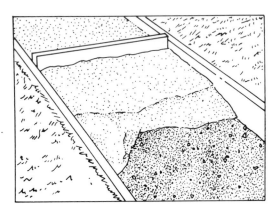

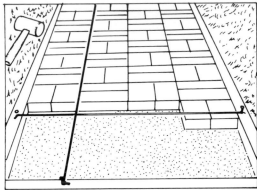

1. Mark out the walk with string and dig 2 inches deeper than the thickness of the brick. Lay an edging of treated 2 by 4s on edge or bricks on end. (Fill brick joints with sand or, for more stability, set in mortar.) Add 2 inches of mason's sand for the base of the path. Level with a board and tamp firmly. (If drainage is a problem, use pea gravel instead of sand.)

2. To keep brick squared and straight when installing, establish horizontal and vertical guidelines with string. Lay the brick and secure in place by tapping gently with a rubber hammer.

3. Spread more sand over the brick, sweeping it into the cracks. Water the surface to settle the sand. When the walk is dry, fill the cracks with sand again. The more firmly the sand is packed between the bricks, the tighter the bricks of the walkway will be. (For a more permanent path, set the bricks in about a ¾-inch bed of mortar, and squeeze mortar between the joints. Then finish by scrubbing mortar over the joints and immediately wash the brick surface clean.)

is easy to work with and an economical choice for do-it-yourself projects. Although it can be set in mortar, the simplest way to lay a brick walk is on a two-inch sand cushion. Roofing felt placed between the brick and sand is optional, but it will help prevent the green staining that is sometimes caused by algae growth. A running-bond pattern allows you to use common brick, which is less expensive than pavers. However, some cutting will be required. For a basket-weave pattern, four-by-eight-inch pavers are a good choice because they can be placed close together and require no cutting. If you live in an area with harsh winter weather, use a hard-burned, severe-weathering brick that will resist cracking. Also, although you may love their mellow

look, be careful when using old bricks. Since the source of the brick is unknown, so is its degree of hardness; it could therefore flake and crack after exposure to rain, snow, or freezing conditions.

Concrete, either poured or cast, makes reliable paving for functional walks. Less costly than brick, it is more interesting when combined with other materials. Four-foot modular blocks, set in gravel or in a lawn, will produce a good-looking walk, as will circles of concrete embedded with pea gravel or pebbles. Concrete stepping-stones can also be used to protect the grass where worn places in the lawn indicate that people are shaping their own paths. With a grid of treated wood and an edging of brick, exposed aggregate concrete provides a color-

ful, nonslip walking surface. Another option is concrete made to look like stone, brick, tile, or wood. Some of this concrete is molded into pavers; another kind consists of patterns stamped into wet concrete. The installation of this *faux* paving is less expensive and faster than real brick.

Flagstone, which is made from rock that has been split into flat pieces for paving, has great appeal for walkways of all types because of its rugged good looks and its natural affinity with the earth. The name "flagstone" refers to many types of paving stones, including bluestone, slate, sandstone, limestone, and granite. Flagstone can be left in rough, random shapes for informal, rustic applications, or it can be cut into uniform sizes for a more structured, architectural look. More costly and difficult to handle than brick, flagstone can be laid on stable soil or in mortar over a sand bed or a concrete foundation.

Stones, big and small, are a fine material for garden walks. They range from small pebbles, which can be set in mortar or laid as a loose aggregate, to large fieldstones (a name used for any unquarried stone found in or on the ground) and cobblestones. Although impervious to weather, some stones can be slippery when wet, and their uneven surface can make them difficult to walk on. They are therefore best used for short paths rather than for utilitarian walks or steps.

Loose aggregates such as wood chips and crushed stone or gravel make fine informal walkways. They are low in cost and easy to apply, but they may need raking and replenishing from time to time. Laying the material within borders of treated wood keeps it from scattering on a lawn. One advantage of loose aggregates is that rain water can run right through them, so drainage is not a problem.

Wood adds an informal quality to the landscape. It is less permanent than brick, concrete, or flagstone, but also less expensive. Redwood, cedar, and cypress rounds can be set in a bed of gravel or smooth stones; blocks cut from big timbers can be laid like bricks; and board lumber can be nailed to runners over sand as an adjunct to a low-level deck. Wood should be treated with preservative to avoid the decay and insect damage that would otherwise result from its contact with the moist ground.

The same rough-cut fieldstone is used here for walkway, retaining wall, and steps, creating an environment that, with roses and other plants growing in profusion, is redolent of a romantic country garden of centuries past.

PATIOS AND DECKS

At the turn of this century, while porches and verandas overlooked gardens located at the front of the house, backyards were often children's play spaces and service areas, accessible from a narrow side or rear door. By the end of the century, however, the role played by the backyard has changed. The fitness movement, the tendency toward informal entertaining, and the enthusiasm for gardening have spawned lap pools, spas, gazebos, cookout centers, and other amenities that contribute to alfresco relaxation and entertainment. Perhaps more than any other outdoor structure, patios and decks—today's outdoor rooms—reflect this increasing emphasis on outside activities.

Before starting on a patio- or deck-building project, study your property, analyzing sun and shade patterns, prevailing winds, good and bad views, noise sources, privacy needs, and lighting requirements. These will all affect your decisions about the style, location, and size of the outdoor room and determine its function. Also, the size and shape of the deck or patio should complement and be in scale with your house, whether it is a small Cape Cod or in a contemporary style with walls of glass.

Patios and decks that face north, receiv-

ing little or no sun, are cool or cold. Those facing south are warmed by the sun for much of the day. On the east, patios and decks remain cool, since they are warmed only by the morning sun. And on the west they may be hot, since they receive the full force of the sun from midafternoon on. The southeast or southwest side of your house usually provides the most pleasing mix of sun and shadow.

Decks and patios should be sited to take advantage of cooling summer breezes but should be out of the path of cold winds that would reduce your pleasure off-season. Also, be aware of microclimates as you plan. While solid privacy walls might block chilly breezes, for example, they may, on the other hand, increase air turbulence.

Think as well about how trees, shrubs, fences, or walls can be used to screen your patio or deck from the street and neighbors. You may also need to provide relief from the hot sun. If trees or a large umbrella don't do the job, you can do it structurally. A shade structure built with lattice will not only diffuse bright sunlight, but will also provide a sense of enclosure, pleasing shadow patterns, and support for climbing vines that will supply further shade. Also, if you live where mosquitoes and gnats are troublesome, a screened structure on part of your deck could make the difference between enjoying and not enjoying your outdoor room after dark.

Work out lighting for your patio or deck during the early planning stages, so that wires can be concealed or buried if

A simple change in materials is often the best way to demarcate the various living spaces of a yard. Here, the switch from the flagstone terrace to durable plantation-grown teakwood decking in this design by Peter Alexander, effectively signals the transition to the pool and spa area that sits cantilevered above a slope.

necessary. Include bright, functional lighting for cooking and games, soft mood lighting for dining, and accent lighting to dramatize any nearby garden features.

PATIOS

Patios and decks are structurally different from one another, so consider the pros and cons of each while doing your research. Patios are built on ground level of masonry materials—brick, flagstone, concrete, and tile. They usually have an intimate quality and offer a sense of shelter and protection. On a busy street, a patio can be a sanctuary surrounded by walls, in the tradition of the inner courtyard of old Spanish and desert Southwest architecture. However, in the country, patios are often expansive spaces, facing panoramic views of a garden, swimming pool, pond, tennis court, or even a sweep of lawn. A patio can also be a shady, quiet retreat in some far-off corner of your property, or a series of terraced platforms with connecting steps. A suburban patio with access to the kitchen makes an ideal spot for entertaining or simple family meals. If you already have an outmoded concrete patio that you tend to ignore, it could be resurfaced, enlarged, or linked to a new patio with the addition of brick or flagstone.

A patio needs a good foundation and surface drainage. It should also be nonskid, nonglare, and flat enough to accommodate your furniture and pots of plants. The most commonly used materials generally satisfy these criteria.

Brick adds elegance and warmth to almost any style of house or landscape. It can be laid in sand or mortared into a concrete slab. A mortarless brick patio is the easiest type to build, since the individual units are simple to handle, and expenditures need not be great. However, such a patio needs a rigid edging to keep the brick from shifting. Brick on-end or treated railroad ties make good-looking border materials. From time to time, a few bricks may need to be replaced or realigned. Brick set in mortar is a more permanent installation.

Brick can be laid in a variety of patterns, including basket weave, herringbone, stack, and running bond, thus offering many design opportunities. Keep the pattern balanced, however, and in harmony with walks and other garden elements. Since a smooth surface can become slippery when wet, choose a rough-textured brick.

Because of its earthy colors and textures, flagstone integrates well with country surroundings and makes a handsome garden floor. Although it can be placed directly on a lawn for use as stepping-stones, for a durable patio, flagstone should be mortared in place on a concrete slab. Since individual shapes are irregular and colors varied, the stones should be selected and laid carefully, so the surface does not become too busy. An uneven surface could pose problems in the placement of furniture, and some types of stone may stain. Flagstone is not as easy to work with as brick, and it is more costly.

Long-wearing and low-cost, concrete is a versatile material for patio construction. This mixture of cement, sand, gravel, and water can be poured on the site or cast in rounds and rectangles that can be laid in sand or mortar. Brick or treated wood used in a grid pattern between blocks and as border detailing will relieve the dullness of a large solid surface. Also to offset its plainness, concrete can be colored and stamped into patterns and textures that simulate brick, stone, or tile, or pebbles and stones can be added to create an exposed aggregate surface. If not properly installed, concrete can crack and buckle in freezing climates.

Outdoor ceramic tile is architectural in feeling and makes handsome patios, particularly when they are extensions of indoor rooms that have tile floors. Larger and thicker than its indoor counterpart, unglazed patio and quarry tile is well-suited to barbecue areas because it is easy to keep clean. Available with a nonskid surface for safety, this durable, decorative material is expensive, particularly since it must be laid correctly in mortar on a level slab.

DECKS

Whereas patios tend to blend with their natural surroundings, decks, which are made of wood, seem more like extensions or structural parts of the house. Extremely versatile, decks can be constructed in many configurations and at any height from ground level up. Their adaptability gives decks exciting design possibilities, potentially adding more drama to the landscape than patios. Decks can be built around a stately old tree or an outcropping of rock. They can convert an unusable hillside into several outdoor rooms, or they can be cantilevered over a high cliff. If your yard is small, a deck can make it seem larger, by articulating the space and adding to its usefulness. Decks can open up virtually all interior spaces to the outdoors, with different decks satisfying various family needs— a sunny area off the family room for the children to play, a quiet spot off the kitchen for dining with friends, a secluded place off the bedroom to stretch out and read the paper, and a big expanse off the living room to entertain a crowd.

From a practical standpoint, decks can solve many problems. Besides leveling off irregular terrain, decks are ideal for land that is sandy or soggy, which is not conducive to patio construction. Also, since wood does not store heat, decks do not get hot

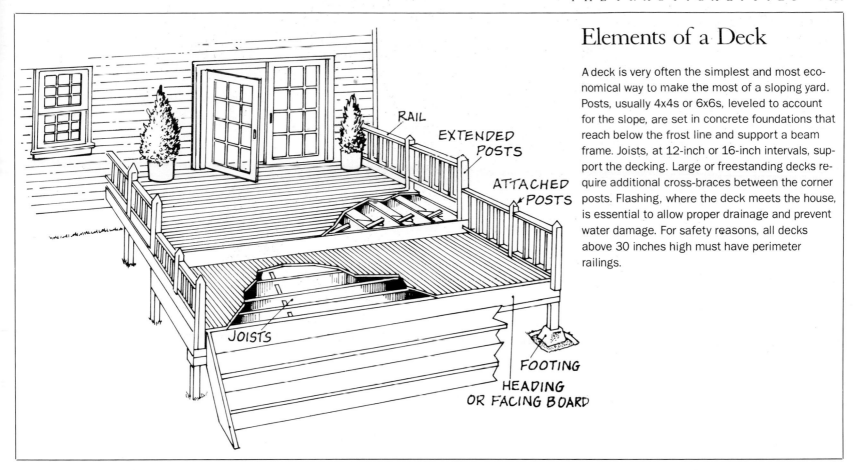

Elements of a Deck

A deck is very often the simplest and most economical way to make the most of a sloping yard. Posts, usually 4x4s or 6x6s, leveled to account for the slope, are set in concrete foundations that reach below the frost line and support a beam frame. Joists, at 12-inch or 16-inch intervals, support the decking. Large or freestanding decks require additional cross-braces between the corner posts. Flashing, where the deck meets the house, is essential to allow proper drainage and prevent water damage. For safety reasons, all decks above 30 inches high must have perimeter railings.

underfoot like masonry can, and they offer a softer surface for toddlers.

Another advantage of decks is that they do not have the excavation and drainage requirements associated with masonry materials. Because of the gaps between the boards, no slope for water runoff is needed. In addition, since boards can be placed on a low framework over an asphalt surface, decks are a practical solution for rooftop terraces. Prefabricated modular deck-squares provide a simple technique for covering up a crumbling concrete slab, if there is one on your property.

Deck construction involves footings, piers, posts, beams, joists, a ledger board if bolted to the house, and the decking or surface boards. The boards can be laid in different patterns: straight, diagonal, her-ringbone, diamond, concentric squares, or basket weave. A common method of installation is to place two-by-six boards parallel to each other at right angles over the joists, which have been spaced on sixteen-inch centers over the supporting understructure. The size and shape of your deck, as well as the board size and pattern, will affect the framing construction.

Although simple patterns are most restful, busier ones do add visual interest to decks. Large decks should have more than one access point from the house, and wide doors are better than small ones. As a matter of fact, one of your initial steps in better relating indoors and out should be to replace a window with a door or to open up a wall to the outdoors with sliding glass units or French doors.

Redwood, cedar, and pressure-treated lumber are common choices for deck flooring. Long-standing staples for garden construction, redwood and cedar are expensive, but their built-in resistance to decay, their natural beauty, and their fine weathering qualities more than compensate for the cost. Using economical garden grades of redwood can help to keep cost down. "Construction heart" is recommended for elements that touch the ground—posts, beams, and joists; "common" is suitable above-ground for decking and trim.

Pressure-treated wood is widely used for deck construction, as it wears well and is the most economical. Usually made of pine or fir, which are not naturally rot resistant, the lumber has been impregnated with chemical preservatives to protect it from

The simple wooden fence adds a Colonial feel to the contemporary structure. Roses spilling over the top of the fence add color.

water, insects, and fungi. Its greenish tint will weather to gray within a year.

All wood will weather naturally to a soft silver gray, but the process can be accelerated with a gray weathering stain. Even if you want the wood to weather on its own, it is beneficial to protect it with a clear water-repellent preservative, one containing a mildew retardant perhaps, which should be reapplied every few years. Stain, either opaque or semitransparent, penetrates the wood and will not need to be reapplied as often as paint, which is a surface coating. Bleach will produce a weathered look over-

night. Make sure the wood is completely dry before any finish is applied. Buy only galvanized nails, which will not corrode and stain the wood. Wood does require more maintenance than masonry to remove mildew or fungus, splinters or discoloration, and to renew its finish.

Railings, benches, steps, and planters are the finishing details that will articulate and add character to your deck. Strong railings, made so that small children cannot fall through or over them, are necessary for decks three feet or more above the ground. Railings should be at least thirty-six inches high, and the seats fourteen inches above the decking with a depth of at least twelve inches. Slim vertical rails will not obstruct

views while you are lounging in your chaise. Wide boards will give you privacy and block undesirable views. A board two-by-six cap-rail will provide a place to lean and put a drink. If your deck is close to the ground, you can use benches instead of railings to define the edges and to provide seating. Benches can be built-in or free-standing, with backs or without.

Steps further integrate the deck with the house and yard. A practical ratio is twelve-inch deep treads and six-inch risers, since a pair of two by sixes can be used for treads and one for the riser. Finally, the crowning touch, perhaps, are planters, which relieve the horizontal surface of a deck and help relate it to the garden areas.

GARDEN STRUCTURES

Pergolas, arbors, trellises, and gazebos play a special role in yard design. Serving both decorative and functional purposes, these architectural elements add a pleasing counterpoint to plantings. Besides contributing height and focal points to the landscape, they provide shade, privacy, plant support, and, most important, a sense of enclosure and protection without sacrificing light and air.

Pergolas are ideal for shading walks that connect one area of the yard with another and for creating shaded outdoor rooms. As "hallways," these open airy structures can be made easily, using four-by-four uprights firmly anchored in the ground, four-by-four beams, and two-by-six cross-pieces. Built in conjunction with a patio as an extension of the house, a pergola creates a sheltered atmosphere for relaxing outdoors, particularly when adorned with vertical lattice panels, hanging plants, and climbing vines. A pergola can also be located away from the house as a freestanding garden retreat, or with a boundary wall or fence serving as part of the enclosure and support.

Arbors or arches are another garden delight. They can be used as a focal point in the distant landscape, as an inviting entranceway to your property, as a frame for a lovely view, and as a "doorway" between different parts of the yard. Commonly made of enameled steel or wood with lattice sides, these time-honored structures sup-

A gazebo forms an outdoor room that is ideal for summer entertaining.

port roses and other climbing plants that will add more charm and shade to your backyard. Allow eight feet for headroom and a width of at least four feet.

Trellises provide a decorative form of screening, shading, and plant support. They can be made of thin, narrow flexible lath, or thicker strips of wood that are nailed together in a diamond or square pattern. The lattice panels are then surrounded by a supporting framework that must be anchored firmly in the ground. Lattice, or trelliswork, is enjoying a renaissance today for the same reason that *treillage* was popu-

Garden Structures

Gazebos, commonly constructed from wood, are freestanding structures, often with lattice or screen walls.

When extending from the side of a house, pergolas are open and airy alternatives to a porch.

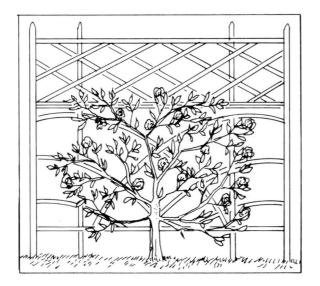

Trellises, which can be constructed in any number of fanciful designs, serve as open walls within a property, defining but not enclosing a space, and incidentally as supports for plants.

Arbors can be little more than arched supports for climbing plants or vines such as wisteria, roses, honeysuckle, or clematis, that shade a walk or patio.

lar in seventeenth-century France. It is appreciated for its own geometric designs, whether simple or intricate, and it achieves spectacular effects with twining plants. A simple trellis can be used to support plants along a fence or the wall of a house. More intricate designs function as walls of outdoor rooms, admitting light, air, and views, and filtering sunlight in an intriguing play of light and shadow. Latticework screens are useful for concealing an unsightly view or a service area, and they can effectively delineate a play space for children. While lath is available in ready-made trellis panels, you can give free reign to your imagination and make your own lattice panels with large or small grids, depending on what effects you want to achieve.

Lattice structures can be made from different woods and finished in a variety of ways. Of course, any wood that comes into contact with the ground must be decay- and rot-resistant. Redwood, cedar, and cypress are inherently resistant and can be left to weather naturally. Pine, on the other hand, must be preservative-treated and should be painted or stained for further protection and aesthetic appeal. White offers a crisp, bright accent in natural surroundings. However, choose a color that complements your house and other garden features.

Gazebos offer another kind of open-air pleasure, with more protection from the elements than pergolas or arbors. Whether assembled from a kit or custom-made, these freestanding structures have airy sides but solid roofs and floors. They can be clean-lined, glass-roofed, and contemporary, or they can be romantic and fanciful, with the gingerbread decorations of their Victorian ancestors. If viewed from the house, a gazebo can be an ornamental feature in the yard. If tucked away in a corner, it can serve as a quiet hideaway—a retreat for reading and viewing nature.

Plantings supply the finishing touch to pergolas, arbors, trellises, and gazebos. Hanging pots of annuals provide colorful blooms. Climbers, such as roses and honeysuckle, add privacy, as well as the fragrance and shade that bring these architectural elements to life. Other possibilities include bittersweet, trumpet vine, clematis, Virginia creeper, silver lace, and wisteria.

Arbors can make ideal transitions from one part of a yard to another. When they are deep, they seem to impel us from one area to the next. When they are essentially archways, they form a dramatic entranceway, and make us want to stop and look before proceeding.

RECREATION AREAS

Well-planned recreation areas encourage outdoor activities that benefit the whole family, physically and mentally. At the same time, they save wear and tear on the rest of the yard. For tots, a play area could consist of a sandbox, swing set, or climbing frame. For older children, it could be a tree house, badminton court, or basketball backboard attached to a garage or pole. And for adults, the recreation area could be a tennis or badminton court or a stretch of lawn designed especially for playing croquet.

For the youngest members of the family, allow lots of elbow room—away from steps—to roll on the grass, play tag, and exercise flights of fantasy. A separate play yard will help keep balls, bikes, and other playtime paraphernalia out of the bushes and flower beds. A sandbox may be built above ground with wide edges to sit on or it can be sunk into the ground. If built above ground, it can be as simple as a five-foot square without a bottom, handy for any repositioning that you might do later on. If you build your own sandbox, use pressure-treated lumber. For an older child, a tree house makes a wonderful hideaway. If your yard lacks appropriate trees in which to build, you can construct support posts around the trunks.

Safety is a major consideration for children's play structures. Wood should be a naturally decay-resistant variety such as redwood, cedar, or cypress. Also recommended is nontoxic CCA (copper chromate arsenate) treated lumber. Stay away from

Making a Simple Sandbox

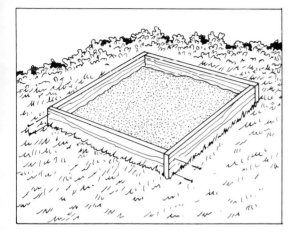

1. Cut and nail a frame, about 4 feet square, from pressure-treated lumber. To improve drainage, put a 2-inch layer of gravel inside the frame.

2. Nail a broad seating edge to the top of the frame and fill the box with 6 inches of fine, washed sand from a masonry supplier or toy store.

Barbecues

creosote-treated woods, which should not be available anyway, since their use for play areas and vegetable gardens has been banned by the Environmental Protection Agency. Also, do not try to treat ordinary lumber yourself, as many preservatives are highly toxic and should not be in contact with humans, pets, or plants. Wood can be left to weather naturally. Make sure all fastenings—nails, nuts, bolts, and washers— are galvanized for rust resistance. Bolts are better than nails for major joints. Footings for a heavy framework or poles should be below the frost line to prevent heaving. Of course, corners should be rounded, nuts and bolts countersunk, and splintery spots sanded smooth. Finally, the ground beneath the play structures should be resilient and free of stones. If not with grass, the area

If the proper safety precautions are taken, recreation areas for children and adults need not be separated from each other. Croquet, for example, uses a soft grass surface. As such, it is the ideal game to situate next to a child's swingset and slide, which also need a soft surface underfoot.

could be covered with a couple of inches of sand or shredded hardwood bark and bordered with landscape timbers.

Recreation areas for grown-up games need lots of space, particularly if they are regulation-size, which is desirable for serious players. An uneven lawn is acceptable for badminton and croquet, games that are becoming popular once again for young and old. For croquet, allot a space about 85 feet long by 37 feet wide, though you can cheat a bit on the dimensions. Thick, closely cropped grass works best. For badminton, you will need a court at least twenty by forty feet large, located out of the wind and away from overhanging branches. A tennis court requires a space of 60 by 120 feet, including the area around the court itself. (A doubles court is thirty-six feet wide and seventy-eight feet long.) And of course a fence to keep the balls in the court is needed as well.

Whether you simply roll a charcoal grill out onto the lawn, set up a table hibachi on a wooden deck, or drop a gas unit into a masonry base on a terrace, open-air cooking is easier and more enjoyable in a spot specifically devoted to it. If you can include storage cabinets, countertops, a sink, a small refrigerator, lighting, and places to eat, you can fashion an inviting kitchen/family room outdoors.

Accessibility to the house simplifies the installation of wiring, plumbing, and gas lines, not to mention the transporting of food, cooking implements, and serving pieces between outside and in. For safety reasons, the cooking areas should be located away from wood fences, walls, overhangs, and tree branches. The barbecue should be placed where smoke is least likely to blow into windows or your neighbor's backyard. If your plans call for electrical, plumbing, or gas tie-ins, you will have to meet local building codes that may require that work be done by a licensed professional.

In designing a barbecue area that will suit the style of your house and landscape, choose materials that will provide visual continuity and yet withstand different weather conditions. For example, redwood for storage cabinets and glazed ceramic tile or granite for countertops are not only good-looking but also waterproof. (Bricks, which collect grease and dirt, are not recommended for countertops.) Other provisions for comfort, day and night, include adequate shade, privacy, and lighting.

SWIMMING POOLS

The backyard pool has advanced far beyond the ubiquitous turquoise rectangle. In years gone by, a pool was simply plunked down in a sunny open space—often as a status symbol—and that was that. Little attempt was made to relate this body of water to the house and surrounding yard. Today, however, pools play a larger role in outdoor activities—they are used not only for family recreation, but for staying fit as well—and their appearance has changed accordingly.

Pools designed for swimming laps, for example, are long, narrow, and only four-feet deep. Many pools have a spa tucked into one corner to soak away the tensions of the day, or a shallow semicircle at one end where children can splash and play games. Others are free-form in shape and have reflective black bottoms that simulate natural ponds. Waterfalls further the illusion, and boulders serve as diving boards.

A pool project should not be taken lightly, because the initial cost is just the beginning. Safety, operation, and maintenance costs must be considered, as should all the extras including decking, furniture, flowers and other plants, fences (a legal requirement), screens to supply privacy and buffer the wind, equipment to test and clean the water, a cover to retain pool heat and keep debris out, a dressing room to reduce traffic through the house, and lighting to provide safety and atmosphere at night. In addition but equally important, bear in mind that a pool will not only dramatically change your landscape, but also your family's pattern of living. Once the pool is in, you cannot return it.

DESIGN AND LOCATION

For entertaining, you will want a large shallow end and a pool surround for sunning, relaxing, and eating. Experts say that a pool measuring at least sixteen by thirty-two feet, with a deep end for diving, will satisfy a full range of needs. The shallow end should be the largest part of the pool space. Steps sited in a corner of the pool will leave the main swimming areas unobstructed, while long, gentle steps can replace a ladder in addition to serving as a place to rest. For splashing and play, a pool needs to be only three feet deep; four to five feet is average. At the deep end, you will need at least eight feet for diving. A thirty-inch-high, ten-foot-long board will suffice for most divers.

For lap swimmers, water to a depth of $3\frac{1}{2}$ to 4 feet is recommended so they do not touch bottom and can turn around easily at the ends. A calisthenics program requires water three to five feet deep. The longer the pool the better, but forty feet is adequate, as is a width or eight to ten feet.

This round pool, designed by Glen Fries, is a highly elegant solution to the problem of siting a swimming pool in a relatively small space. Water spilling from the spa into a shallow copper bowl and on into the pool not only links spa to pool but adds movement to the composition. Further movement is created by the rounded pool steps in warm-toned, crab-orchard stone and in the sweeping curves of the brick retaining walls.

The key in planning is to make your pool just large enough to suit your needs. If four or five feet of water for swimming and water games is sufficient, build the pool with only that depth. The more water in the pool, the more energy demands are placed on your equipment.

When thinking about your pool's location, study the sun and wind patterns on your property, as you will want direct sunlight for as much of the day as possible, and you will want to shield the pool from strong breezes. Although trees and shrubs will break the wind and help retain heat in the pool, if they are too close, blowing and falling leaves can be a problem. Nearby neighbors, views, street noise, access to water and utility lines, and the supervision of children are other considerations in selecting a site. In addition, proximity to lot lines or a septic system will affect placement, so zoning regulations should be checked.

MATERIALS

Once you have decided on your pool's use and location, consider materials, size, and shape. By and large, pools are vinyl-lined or made of fiberglass or Gunite. To construct a vinyl-lined pool, which is the most economical type, a frame of aluminum, steel, plastic, concrete block, or treated wood is erected at the pool site. The bottom of the pool is covered with a mixture of sand and cement or vermiculite. The flexible liner is then attached to the supporting frame, and the top of the liner is secured by a special coping that gives the pool a finished look. Available in a range of sizes, shapes, colors, and patterns, the vinyl liners should last ten to fifteen years before needing to be replaced. Minor tears can by repaired without draining.

More expensive than vinyl-lined pools but less costly than those made of Gunite, fiberglass pools are constructed of one-piece, preformed shells that are lowered into a prepared foundation over a bed of sand contoured to fit the shell. They are durable, easy to clean, and resistant to algae growth. Their limited shapes and sizes are a disadvantage, however. "Hybrid" pools, composed of fiberglass walls with bottoms of vinyl or concrete, offer increased flexibility.

Gunite, a cement mixture, is the most costly, most durable, and most flexible material for pools, affording complete freedom in custom sizes and shapes. The Gunite is sprayed from a hose onto a foundation of steel rods formed against the earth. The interior is then finished with a fine coat of plaster. Pigment from white to black can be added to the plaster. Choose white for clear, sparkling blue water, and dark gray or black finishes for the look of a reflecting pool or natural pond. In addition to offering visual depth, the dark finishes retain solar heat better than light colors do, and they hide chlorine discoloration. A band of tile along the water line will facilitate the removal of minerals, oil, and dirt.

MAINTENANCE

The pool builder's price usually includes the basic equipment required to operate the pool—pump, filter, skimmer, steps or ladder, and minimal decking—but do clarify exactly what is in the contract. Since clean water, free from harmful bacteria and algae, is a chief requisite for pool enjoyment, maintenance will be a primary—and ongoing—cost and concern. The pool's support system (pump, filter, skimmer, and so on) will take care of most of this, and automatically if you want. You will also have to be sure that the chemical balance of the

water is right. Test kits are available to help maintain the correct alkaline level (pH) and the necessary level of residual disinfectant for fresh and healthful water.

Heating is an extra that can increase pool enjoyment in many climates. Electricity, gas, oil, and solar energy are all possible methods of heating. Some are more economical than others, depending on where you live. Since conventional fuel costs are high, it makes sense to capitalize on the sun's free heat. Although the initial investment for an active system is large, it is practical if you have a south-facing roof to install the collectors and you receive full sunlight. Simply stated, a pump circulates pool water through the solar collectors on the roof and back to the pool again. Some back-up heating may still be needed, however. Also effective are passive solar systems, which conserve heat already in the pool, although a pool cover, a dark bottom, and landscaping that buffers the wind will also act as heat conservers.

Whether you heat your pool or not, a cover is a wise investment—necessary in winter climates—not only to protect the pool off-season, but to prevent unauthorized use, to keep out dirt and leaves, to retain heat, to reduce evaporation, and to save on cleaning and chemicals. If properly maintained, most pools do not need draining and refilling every year. Several types of covers are available for solar, safety, and winterizing purposes. Bubble plastic, which floats on the water's surface, absorbs heat by day and retains it at night. Less expensive polyethylene will keep out dirt and leaves, but will not hold the heat in well. Mesh covers, held in place in the pool's deck, are effective for safety and winterizing.

It is the finishing touches that will integrate your pool with the rest of your yard—decking, fencing, plantings, and any struc-

Pool Shapes

When planning a pool to suit your site, consider the alternatives to the standard rectangle. Many shapes are possible, and often preferable for specific sites.

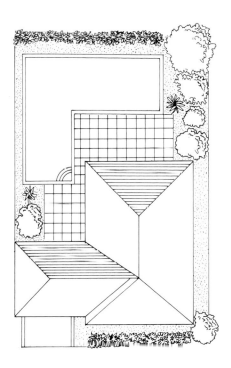

An 'L-shaped' pool can maximize the area for swimming.

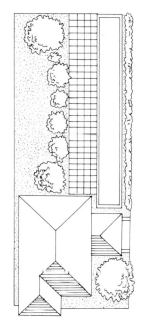

Lap pools can take full advantage of the limited space of a long, narrow property, or can be sited to leave room for other yard features.

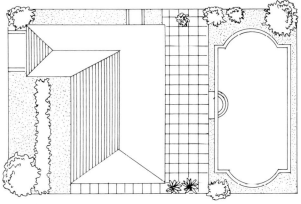

Rounded ends soften the traditional rectangle.

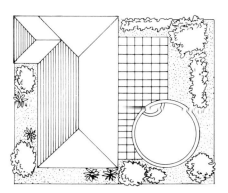

A circular pool tends to play down the rectangular quality of a square lot.

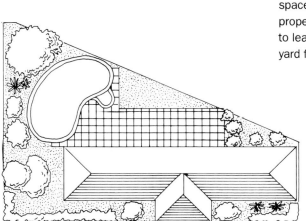

A kidney-shaped pool will capitalize on the space in an awkward, wedge-shaped, or corner lot.

Naturalistic pools can relieve a very angular or wedge-shaped property.

Choosing a Pool Professional

The building of a swimming pool involves such diverse areas of expertise in design, siting, soil, materials, construction, and landscaping that the services of a professional are crucial. Architects, landscape architects, landscape designers, landscape contractors, and pool contractors are all qualified for the job.

Architects and landscape architects will make sure your swimming pool is aesthetically pleasing and structurally sound. They will undertake the whole project from the design concept and siting to the selection of a good contractor and supervision of construction. A landscape architect's education is best suited to pool surrounds and planting, which are invaluable in a successful design.

A landscape designer's knowledge and credentials are more variable. This person may be more experienced in horticulture and design than in construction, or vice-versa. However, if a landscape designer is also a pool or landscape contractor, he or she can handle the designing, landscaping, and the actual work.

A pool contractor specializes in pool building and a landscape contractor in garden construction. Both are responsible for the entire project and both design, build, and landscape. Major pool-building companies have creative design departments, but may lack comprehensive horticultural know-how. For this specialization, it is better to turn to the landscape architect or landscape designer.

To choose the professional who is right for you, collect recommendations from satisfied pool owners, or get names in your area from organizations such as the Association of Landscape Architects or the National Spa and Pool Institute. And, do not forget your local Chamber of Commerce.

tures you add for entertaining, shade, storage, or dressing. Decking creates a frame for your pool and should blend with any other paved areas in your landscape. Many materials qualify for this surround, which should not be slippery. Flagstone suits woodsy, country surroundings; brick lends a more formal, elegant air; wood has a casual, contemporary flavor. A pebble aggregate is less slippery than plain concrete and less heat-absorbing. If overheated concrete is a problem, cool decking can be applied to reduce surface temperature and to keep bare feet from burning. Granite also remains cool underfoot.

HOT TUBS AND SPAS

With their therapeutic heat and swirling waters pumped through hydro-jets, spas and hot tubs have become part of many backyards. Although they do the same thing, spas and hot tubs are quite different in appearance. Hot tubs are natural and rustic. Usually round or oval and made of

Gentle steps leading into shallow water are easier and safer to use than a traditional ladder, and are also convenient places to sit. These substantial granite steps take on a shimmering, weightless quality when viewed from above.

redwood, they are also available in other shapes and in such woods as teak, cedar, oak, cypress, and mahogany. A standard five-foot-wide by four-foot-deep tub holds about five hundred gallons of water and provides seating for four adults. Spas are sleek and more contemporary. Those made of molded fiberglass have either a gelcoat or acrylic finish. Gelcoat, which is less costly than acrylic but more susceptible to color fading and corrosion, will need more routine care and will have to be resurfaced after about five years. Acrylic's hard surface is resistant to scratches and maintains its color indefinitely. Plastic spas come in many sizes, shapes, and colors. A standard spa is four feet deep by five to six feet in diameter. Custom-made Gunite spas are usually attached to swimming pools, and they can be designed in any shape or size you want.

GARDEN POOLS

A garden pool or pond, whether simple or complex, will add a strong structural form and a dramatic focal point to your yard. Yet it is the subtle, sensuous aspect of water that satisfies most. Still, clear water exudes peace and tranquility as it mirrors images of the changing sky and neighboring greenery. Water flowing from a fountain or waterfall supplies "music" and varies the patterns and colors that sunlight produces as it plays over the water's surface. Exotic aquatic plants provide another kind of magic as their blossoms unfold and perfume the air. And finally, the opportunity to learn and be entertained by watching pond life is an ongoing delight in itself.

FORMAL POOLS

When deciding what kind of pool will fit in with your yard and way of life, first establish whether you want a formal or informal look. A formal pool, which often accompanies a patio, has a rigid, geometric shape—a square, rectangle, circle, or hexagon, for example. This style is suitable for most settings as long as it is in scale with the surroundings. A fountain and gentle waterfall are ideal accessories for a formal pool. If you include a fountain, keep the jet simple and not too high, or windblown spray could be a problem. A small flow of water between level changes in a formal pool will add a pleasing vertical contrast to the horizontal sheet of water. A submersible pump can be used to recirculate the water of both

the fountain and the waterfall, and the power source could be used to connect waterproof lights for nighttime enjoyment. If the pool is raised rather than sunken, the rim offers an inviting spot to sit.

A formal pool is usually professionally built of waterproof concrete, with a drain for occasional cleaning and an overflow outlet to prevent flooding in a heavy rain. If built in a freezing climate, the concrete should be reinforced, and the sides should be sloped to allow ice to expand upwards. Concrete construction also permits you to build in a shelf for plants and stepping-stones, which should look as though they were floating on the water. Edgings are an important design detail to finish off the pool. Whether made of concrete, brick, paving stones, or landscape timbers, they should overhang the water by at least two inches, so the shadow of the overhang will hide any scum that might stain the rim as the water evaporates.

INFORMAL POOLS

Informal pools take free-form shapes reminiscent of the contours of a natural pond or bog. They are usually sited away from the house and require plant life that simulates a natural habitat. Remember that such water gardening needs an appropriate balance of plant, fish, and animal life to be completely successful. This balance is achieved by combining the right plant species with the right number and type of aquatic animals.

Oxygenating plants such as submerged grasses keep the water clear by retarding algae growth, and they provide food and shelter for the fish. Bog plants make a natural camouflage at the pond's edge. These marginal aquatic plants grow in shallow areas, and their leaves and flowers emerge above the water's surface. Hardy types include arrowhead, arum, common cattail, flowering rush, water iris, dwarf papyrus, bog lily, water poppy, water canna, and cardinal flower. Floating aquatics such as water chestnut, water lettuce, and water hyacinth shade the water's surface and also aid in algae control. Water lilies and lotus are the ornamentals that produce the bold, beautiful flowers most often seen on a pond's surface. They keep the water cool, retard oxygen loss, and provide a haven for fish. Lilies are grouped into hardy and tropical varieties. The hardy types will live for many years, while the tropical ones are seasonal in a cold climate. In a man-made pool, lilies and lotus should be grown in soil-filled containers submerged in the water. Although fish, fresh-water clams, snails, and frogs aren't necessary, they do add to the fascination of pond life. In addition, they help control algae growth and keep the mosquito population under control. Their waste provides natural fertilizer for the pool's plants. Among the golden carp—commonly known as goldfish—orfes and Japanese koi are popular; others include calicoes, comets, black moors, and fantails.

A bridge will help integrate your pond with the rest of the yard. It will also permit a path to take a logical course rather than

Building a Lily Pond

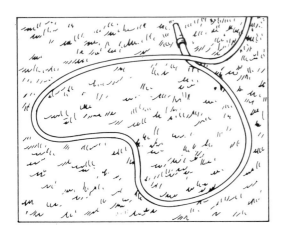

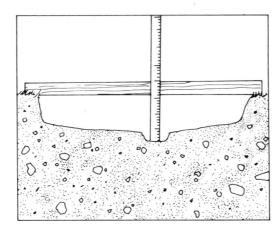

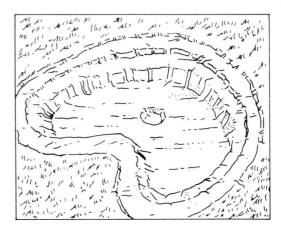

1. Use a piece of clothesline or a garden hose to lay out the pool's outline in a naturalistic shape. Estimate the pool-liner size by measuring the length and width at the widest and longest points of your outline. To each dimension, add twice the pool's planned depth plus 12 extra inches for the overlap at the edges.

2. Dig a hole 1 inch deeper than your planned depth to allow for a cushioning layer of fine sand or damp newspaper. Place a board across the excavation and check the depth with a yardstick to make sure it is right. If you are adding a submersible pump, dig out a pocket for it in the center.

3. If you wish, cut ledges for bog plants, 9 to 12 inches wide and 6 inches below the rim on one or more sides. Cut a shallow ledge 8 to 10 inches wide in the grass around the perimeter to act as a seat for edging stones or bricks.

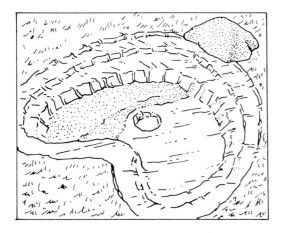

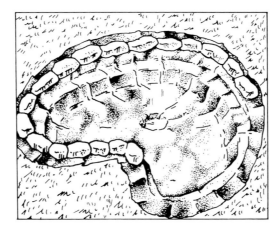

4. Remove from the hollow any stones or protruding roots that would puncture the vinyl, and line with at least 1 inch of cushioning damp newspaper or fine builder's sand.

5. Place the liner in position so that it overlaps evenly on all sides. Hold the liner in place by weighting the edges with bricks or smooth stones.

6. Fill the pond with water to 2 inches below the rim and allow the liner to settle. Trim the excess liner, leaving 6 to 8 inches to anchor under stones, bricks, or paving blocks set around the perimeter. (For a more permanent installation, edge with flat stones set in mortar over a bed of gravel and grout the joints.)

The formal look of a rectilinear garden pool is more suitable for a patio or courtyard than for a lawn. This rectangular pool, which is flush with the surrounding patio, echoes in shape the planting beds in the courtyard and even the bench that sits, centered behind the pool, against the fence. A fountain adds movement and splashing sounds, and water plants contribute color and organic shapes.

going around the body of water. Keep the span of a bridge to no more than four feet, and make sure it is firmly built and anchored so there is no danger of collapse.

Although a fountain would look out of place in an informal pool, a trickle of water over rocks, simulating a mountain stream, would be appropriate.

Pond-like pools are inexpensive, build-it-yourself projects if they are made with heavy-duty polyvinyl chloride (PVC) liners, which are available through water-garden supply companies. Fiberglass is another practical pool material, and can be used for either a formal or informal design. Leak-proof and long-lasting, rigid pre molded fiberglass shells are manufactured in a variety of shapes, though sizes are limited, and the shells are more costly than PVC liners.

LOCATION AND DESIGN

Siting your pool is a major consideration, as is safety. Even a shallow garden pool can be a hazard to young children. A small, decorative pool should be visible from your house, patio, or deck. You will also want the background and reflections to be pleasing. If you put in a fountain or waterfall, you will need a power source to operate the pump. (Make sure all boxes and connections are waterproof.) If you add water plants and fish, the pool must get five to six hours of sunlight a day and should be located away from deciduous trees. (When leaves fall and

sink to the bottom, they will decompose and poison the fish.) In addition, you may want a hose outlet nearby for draining and filling the pool. Chlorinated tap water is dangerous to fish, however. Unless you have well water, allow your tap water to stand for four or five days before adding it to the pool. You may want to include a filter to remove excess sediment and debris.

A garden pool does not have to be deep. One foot to eighteen inches is adequate, unless you are including plants, fish, and animal life, in which case twenty-four inches is recommended, particularly if the fish are to winter over under a coat of ice. However, in most areas of the country you will hit rock after digging about twelve inches, so you may have to plan on a shallower depth. Finishing the sides with waterproof black paint will make a shallow pool look deeper. Also, keep the shape relatively regular to facilitate digging.

Even though the idea of a water garden

in a natural-looking pond is both admirable and enticing, it does entail work to establish and maintain the ecological balance that is necessary for such a pond's survival. Provision must always be made to keep the water free of the algae that stains the pool and clouds the water. Oxygenating plants, snails, and fish create a food chain that will do this naturally. Otherwise, a recirculating pump can be installed in the pool to keep the water from becoming stagnant.

OUTDOOR LIGHTING

There is no reason to stop using the yard when the sun goes down, for landscape lighting is available in types and styles to suit any property. Moreover, while the functional roles of outdoor lighting—security, after-dark use of a patio, safety on steps—are taken for granted, such lighting also offers a wide range of aesthetic satisfactions. The interplay of light and shadow, for example, can assume many moods, from the soft and romantic look of gently moving leaves and tree branches to dramatic and evocative highlights on a textured wall or garden sculpture. If properly illuminated, shrubbery, grass, rocks, paths, and a pool or pond will take on an enchanting glow at night. In addition, general ambient lighting can make a house seem larger. Instead of black reflective panes of glass at night, there will be a round-the-clock view to enjoy.

When designing outdoor lighting, draw a plan of your lot with notations of what you want to illuminate. Lighting for safety and security comes first—entrances, walkways, steps, driveway, garage, service areas, and any obstacles or changes in level that are difficult to see in the dark. Personal preferences play a larger role in decorative and mood lighting. You may want to illuminate a large tree, an expanse of ground cover, a piece of garden statuary, or any other areas or objects that could benefit from the drama of night lighting. Such judicious lighting will in fact enhance your entire yard. Just remember that a little light goes a long way at night, so avoid overlighting and do not light everything to the same degree or in the end nothing will stand out.

Lighting professionals strive for the natural look of moonlight or filtered sunlight. Avoiding glare is also important because you do not want to illuminate people, but the surfaces underfoot. Use shielded fixtures, which direct light away from viewers' eyes, or place your lighting out of sight lines, either high or low. Neighbors are another consideration, and care should be taken not to install fixtures where unwanted light will reflect on their house or land.

As a basic guideline, outdoor lighting fixtures should be as inconspicuous as possible, unless they are specifically designed to be decorative, as are postlights next to entrances and flower-shaped fixtures next to paths. Always think of the effect of the light first, rather than the look of the fixture. Before installing your lights, go outside with extension cords, ladders, and portable lights and experiment with different effects.

LIGHTING EFFECTS

Lighting effects can be achieved in various ways and with a variety of bulbs and fixtures, but all lighting is essentially downlighting or uplighting. With downlighting, fixtures mounted high on trees and buildings, or low next to a path, point downward. They can be floodlights or shaded fixtures such as the popular pagoda, mushroom, and bollard styles. Garden paths are best lit with downlighting, either with a spread of illumination or in small patches, depending on the fixture selected. A hidden spotlight shining down from high above the ground can create the effect of moonlight filtering through the trees and casting soft shadows on the ground below.

Lighting from below is called uplighting. It should be used sparingly, as it creates focal points and more theatrical effects than downlighting. Spotlights and well lights sunk in the ground can be used to accent a special tree or shrub. When used to project the pattern of plantings against a wall or fence, it is called "shadowing."

With another technique known as background lighting, uplights, downlights, or a combination of both are used to illuminate walls, fences, or other vertical surfaces. Such "wallwashing" can be a deterrent to prowlers· if it eliminates hiding places. In cross lighting, two or more up- or down-floods or spots beam across a subejct, such as a garden sculpture, from different directions to give it more depth and dimension than a single light source would. If you have a pool or pond, you can angle your lights so that plantings and structures are reflected in the surface of the water. This is known as "mirror lighting."

ELECTRICAL SYSTEMS

Outdoor lighting can be accomplished with standard 110-volt or 12-volt systems. It is, however, low voltage that has made decorative and mood lighting so accessible and affordable. With these systems, a transformer plugged into a 120-volt, grounded

Lighting Trees

Accent lighting is an effective means of dramatizing a favorite tree or stand of trees, and it can be used in a variety of ways with both uplights and downlights. For the best effects, accent lighting should be used sparingly and light sources should be concealed.

Positioning a light source behind a tree emphasizes its form by creating a silhouette effect.

A well light or spotlight can be positioned to throw silhouettes against a wall or a fence.

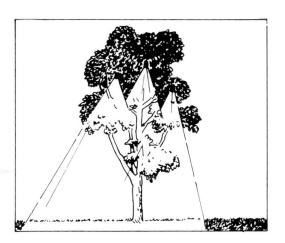

Mounting a fixture—or fixtures—high in a tree, and allowing the light to filter down will mimic moonlight and provide gentle illumination for a ground cover or walk.

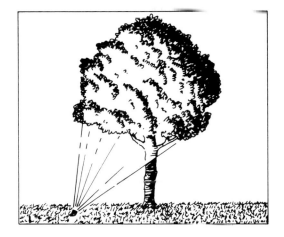

Angling a surface-mounted or recessed spotlight in the ground close to a tree will throw light across the bark and highlight texture, shadows, and contours. Alternatively, directing a spotlight upward into the foliage creates a pleasant play of light and shadow that is particularly effective as breezes blow through the branches.

Beams of light crossing from opposite directions will soften shadows in a stand of trees and emphasize their three-dimensional forms.

Lighting for Safety and Security

You do not need bright, glaring floodlights for nighttime safety and security: Low levels of light can be just as effective when properly placed. To identify visitors, light an entrance with wall-mounted fixtures that illuminate steps, keyholes, and house numbers. Use post lights at entry walks and driveways, not only to increase safety but to add decorative interest as well. To ensure safe footing on steps and paths, install low mushroom or bollard fixtures that spread and diffuse the light. To discourage prowlers, mount single or double floodlights high on a house or garage and at other vulnerable areas, but be sure they are not pointed at drives, walks, and entrances, where they could interfere with a visitor's vision. For added security, consider automatic timers—photocells that automatically turn lights on at dusk and off at daylight—and infrared motion sensors that turn lights on when someone passes in front of them.

outlet reduces the current to a safe 12 volts. Ideal for do-it-yourselfers and those on a budget, low-voltage lighting does not require an electrician to do expensive wiring, unless an outdoor hookup is needed. It also eliminates the need to dig deep trenches for the cable and any danger of electric shock. Kits that include four to six fixtures, cable, and a transformer simplify the job even further. Moreover, if your lighting needs change, the fixtures can easily be relocated. Since low voltage does not use much electricity, it is also kind to your energy bills. (For instance, eight 18-watt low-voltage lights use less energy than one 150-watt floodlight.) Even though low voltage does mean less illumination, and is recommended for soft to medium light, it is appropriate for many applications, since one of the dangers of outdoor lighting is too much brightness.

Standard 110-volt systems are recommended for safety and security where high light levels are needed, such as for game courts and for large acreage. High light level systems can be modified with dimmers. More costly than a 12-volt system, they are also more permanent and tend to need less maintenance. A licensed electrician must do the installation. In many situations, a combination of both systems gives the best results.

FIXTURES

In choosing outdoor fixtures, look for rugged, rustproof styles that will complement your house, and finishes that will withstand fertilizers and weathering. The selection of bulbs—or lamps, as they are referred to in the trade—depends on what you are lighting. A wide variety of incandescents for standard and low-voltage fixtures is offered in various wattages to produce whatever effects you want. The most common is the familiar "A" bulb, which throws light in all directions and is used for different kinds of shielded fixtures. For more fine-tuning, select a reflector bulb, designated as "R," "ER," (for elliptical reflector), and "PAR" (for parabolic aluminum reflector, also known as sealed beam). Made for 110- and 12-volt systems, PAR bulbs are especially popular for spotlighting and floodlighting. They cast light in only one direction and are sold with different beam spreads. Another option are halogen bulbs, which have a brighter, more intense light and a more precise beam-control for specific tasks or accenting. Fluorescents are not often used in garden lighting because of the flat, unflattering color of their light.

WATERING SYSTEMS

The typical suburban image of a homeowner standing on the lawn with a garden hose, or of a sprinkler rhythmically watering lawn and flower bed, is to a great degree a thing of the past. Fortunately, the hose has been replaced by sophisticated sprinkling systems that not only do the job better but free you from this time-consuming task.

SPRINKLER SYSTEMS

Automatic underground sprinklers have almost eliminated the chore of watering lawns and shrub borders. The installation of such sprinklers, which consist of a buried plastic pipe and pop-up heads, is expensive and requires a good water supply. However, since the system uses only the amount of water needed at the appropriate place and time, the water is not wasted, and installation costs are usually offset by lower water bills. Moreover, lawns are not damaged by the installation of such a system, as marks left by trenches and pipe-pulling equipment disappear quickly. The control box allows you to set each sprinkler zone to be on anywhere from several minutes to over an hour, and to time differing irrigation needs in various parts of the yard. On a half acre, for instance, one controller can handle up to six zones with several sprinkler heads in each. Additional controllers and zones would be needed for larger acreage. One great advantage of a timed system is that it can be programmed to operate between 4:00 and 6:00 A.M., when water pressure is highest, wind is minimal, and water loss by evaporation is negligible. The addition of a moisture-sensing device is recommended to shut down the system during rainy weather and return it to normal operation when the soil is dry. Maintenance of underground sprinklers consists of periodic checking of the heads for clogs and adjusting of the timers as weather and water needs change.

Above-ground sprinklers, which attach to the end of a hose, are practical for small areas and newly seeded lawns. Stationary heads, available with different spray patterns, are the least expensive and the simplest to use. Oscillating sprinklers swing back and forth to supply gentle, even watering. The high arc of water the sprinklers deliver means that some water will be blown away by the wind or lost to evaporation. Rotary sprinklers come with an arm that adjusts the distance the sprinkler will throw the water or with a spinning baffle that distributes the water. Impulse sprinklers shoot a circular pattern of water close to the ground and can be adjusted to change the size of the circle or to divide it into quadrants. Traveling sprinklers rely on water pressure to move the head along a guide hose. Above-ground sprinklers can also be equipped with timing systems and moisture-sensors.

DRIP IRRIGATION

Since plants benefit from not getting their leaves wet, and by not becoming stressed through alternate wet and dry cycles, drip-irrigation systems are ideal for vegetable gardens, flower beds, trees, and shrubs. One system, known as a soaker hose, "weeps" water through its entire length. The other consists of plastic tubes and small, movable emitters that are placed next to the plants to be watered. Although soaker hoses are easier to install, they have a faster, less efficient water flow than emitters, and the moisture is not directed at specific plants. Because emitters can become clogged, they should be checked from time to time. Both types of drip-irrigation systems deliver water slowly but steadily, and since the flow is so gentle, they can be used to cover long distances without losing water pressure. Also, since water goes directly to the roots, none is wasted.

Time clocks and moisture sensors can be added to drip systems, as can fertilizer injectors. Once installed, either underground or above ground with a mulch cover, drip systems can remain in place and upkeep should be minimal.

No matter which irrigation system you use, it is usually better to give lawn and plants an occasional deep watering rather than frequent sprinklings. Surface sprinkling results in shallow roots, which can easily scorch in the hot sun, while soaking the soil encourages a healthy root system.

WORKING WITH A PROFESSIONAL

Yard planning—particularly a complete renovation—can benefit greatly from the expertise of a professional. Whether you turn the entire project over to someone else or do the actual work yourself, the training and experience of a landscape professional can be invaluable in solving problems you could not, creating a design you never considered, and introducing materials you never knew about. In other words, professionals can help you avoid mistakes and can save you money in the short and long run. These landscape professionals fall into three categories: landscape architects, landscape designers, and landscape contractors.

LANDSCAPE ARCHITECTS

A landscape architect is a state-licensed professional with a bachelors' or masters' degree. Specially educated in horticulture, building, and design, he or she is the one to turn to if the project is extensive and requires much earth moving, as in the construction of a swimming pool, the building of a multilevel deck, or the basic alteration of a landscape. For a complete project, the architect's responsibilities would include initial sketches, finished drawings to scale, material specifications, plant-material lists, cost estimates, and supervision of the work that is done. Although landscape architects would prefer doing a job from design concept to completion, they are usually available for consultation on an hourly basis. They will also assist you in choosing the right contractor for the job at a reasonable rate.

If you do not want the landscape architect to follow through on the project for budgetary or other reasons, you can use the detailed drawings and specifications yourself and do your own landscaping. This preliminary, overall planning permits you to complete a project in stages if you cannot afford to do it all at once.

LANDSCAPE DESIGNERS

A landscape designer also has special knowledge and training in horticulture and design, but is not licensed. His or her degree of expertise and knowledge may be more variable than that of a landscape architect, but this does not mean that a landscape designer cannot provide the assistance that you want—and for a lower fee. Also not to be forgotten is your local nursery, which may well have someone on staff who is skilled in landscape planning. This person is no doubt knowledgeable about plant materials, and the specific conditions in your locality, and his or her advice is often free.

LANDSCAPE CONTRACTORS

Landscape contractors will implement the plans conceived by the landscape architect or designer (or by you), much as a general contractor does with an architect's plans. They will hire the specialized contractors necessary to do the various jobs—grading, carpentry, pool building, driveway construction, or electrical work, for instance. Landscape contractors are experienced in what happens when and can properly mesh various aspects of the project. However, though experienced in garden construction, a contractor may lack design expertise. Still, his or her services maybe preferable to being your own general contractor and subcontracting for the jobs that need to be done, which takes a lot of coordination and can be troublesome.

To determine who can aid you best, you should have a good idea of what you want to accomplish and how much money you want to spend. By all means match the complexity of the job with the appropriate level of training. Also, before you choose a professional, compare several bids and ask for and check references. Moreover, many garden projects require a permit, and maybe a variance, particularly if they relate to set-back requirements, special zoning ordinances, structural work, and electrical changes. To check on all of this, call your local building inspector's office. Finally, no matter how small the job, always have a letter of agreement or contract that clearly states what everyone's responsibilities are. The letter or contract should spell out the services to be rendered, the exact materials to be used, costs, payment agreement, schedule of work, clean-up arrangements, and completion date.

GARDEN

BASICS

Hardiness Zone Map

This map, produced by the United States Department of Agriculture, divides the North American continent into eleven "hardiness zones," showing the average minimum temperatures that can be expected in each. When you know your hardiness zone you can look in nursery catalogues and so on for those plants that will survive your winters. However, while the map is important as a general guide, it is not infallible. The transitions from one zone to another, for example, are not as firmly fixed as might appear on the map. A number of plants recommended for one zone will do well in the southern region of the next colder zone as well as in the next warmer zone. Furthermore, in certain areas, such as near lakes, in the mountains, or at the edges of large cities, as well as along the boundaries between zones, the climate can vary half a zone within a few miles.

A plant's specific hardiness rating indicates the zone in which it will flourish in optimal health and appearance. Many plants will grow one zone north of their rating but may well suffer some winter damage or fail to flower.

There are also many other factors to consider besides hardiness rating when determining a plant's suitability for your area: Heat and drought resistance, disease resistance, light needs, reliable dormancy, and soil preference are all important.

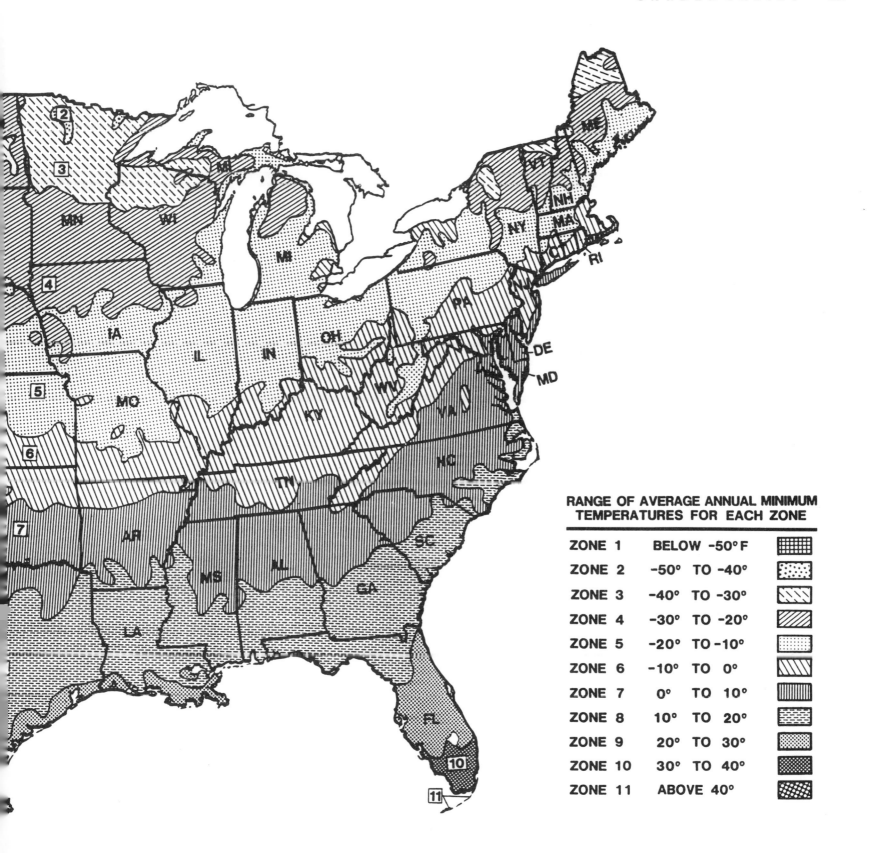

RANGE OF AVERAGE ANNUAL MINIMUM TEMPERATURES FOR EACH ZONE

ZONE 1	BELOW –50°F	
ZONE 2	–50° TO –40°	
ZONE 3	–40° TO –30°	
ZONE 4	–30° TO –20°	
ZONE 5	–20° TO –10°	
ZONE 6	–10° TO 0°	
ZONE 7	0° TO 10°	
ZONE 8	10° TO 20°	
ZONE 9	20° TO 30°	
ZONE 10	30° TO 40°	
ZONE 11	ABOVE 40°	

LAWNS AND GROUNDCOVERS

Lawns play a significant part in our shared experience, as they serve many purposes, both aesthetic and utilitarian. Their color and texture please the senses, and no other surface is quite so satisfactory for recreation. A small yard feels more spacious with a generous expanse of lawn. Grass also absorbs air pollutants and traps dust and on a hot day it has a cooling effect on its surroundings and will reduce glare.

LAWN MAINTENANCE

More and more gardeners are starting and maintaining their lawns organically in order to counteract ground and water pollution, which are exacerbated by the use of chemical fertilizers. It is especially important to follow the steps outlined below if you want to do this. It may be necessary to develop new attitudes and to look at your yard in a different way. A smaller lawn and low-maintenance program is one approach to cutting down on chemicals. High maintenance and close management often require the use of increasing amounts of chemicals without correcting basic problems. Ironically, instead of helping, too many fertilizers, herbicides, insecticides, and fungicides can destroy beneficial bacteria, upset the soil's natural balance, and contribute significantly to the contamination of soil and water.

Developing the right soil, selecting named varieties of disease- and insect-resistant grass seed, using natural fertilizers,

Seeding a Lawn

1. When grading in preparation for a new lawn, avoid low spots, where water can collect, or high spots, which will be scalped when mowing. Too steep a slope can lead to erosion: A drop of not more than one foot in three is recommended.

2. Organic matter should be distributed evenly in the top four to six inches of topsoil, where the root zone is. This will improve soil structure and water-holding capacity.

3. Spread the grass seed evenly but beware of over-seeding which will crowd and ultimately weaken the seedlings.

4. Rake in your grass seed lightly. Too much pressure will cover the seeds too deeply or remove some of them, leaving bare spots. Cover the seed so that about ten percent is visible.

watering properly, and mowing correctly can do a lot to decrease the need for chemicals in maintaining a healthy lawn and in controlling weeds, insects, and diseases. Also, pruning shrubs to increase air flow and trimming trees to reduce shade will likely reduce the need for chemicals. Fertilize once a year instead of twice. You may have to tolerate a few more weeds and an occasional dead patch in your lawn, but it is in the cause of clean earth and water.

The best time to fertilize a lawn is September to October, with a second feeding in April, if you feel it is necessary. If the lawn needs lime for proper acidity, that should also be added in the fall or early spring. Lawns need a balanced mixture of nitrogen, phosphorus, and potassium. The first number on a bag of complete fertilizer represents the proportion of nitrogen, which promotes growth and deep green color; the second number represents phosphorus, which helps lawns develop a strong root system; and the third represents potassium, which gives lawns disease- and drought-resistance. For new lawns, choose a fertilizer with a high proportion of phosphorus; for spring feeding of an established lawn, choose one with lots of nitrogen. Do not overfeed, which can damage grass and, as noted above, often contributes to groundwater pollution. Follow the recommendations on the bag. And remember that slow-release, natural fertilizers are readily available to the gardener interested in growing grass without damaging the environment.

A quick, easy way to apply fertilizer is with a broadcast or rotary spreader. If using a drop-type model, which is recommended for grass seed, overlap the rows slightly to avoid gaps, which cause stripes in the lawn. (Beware of too much overlap, however, as this can cause overgreening or fertilizer burn.) Renting spreaders and other lawn-care equipment is practical, as the machines will be kept in good repair by the dealer and you can get the item that will do the best job when needed.

Regular mowing encourages a healthy lawn. It is better to mow at a higher height, around 2½ inches, than a lower one. In any case, do not keep your grass less than 1½ inches high. If your lawn is scalped, no root system can develop, since roots grow to a depth that is about the same as the height of the blades of grass. Long roots search out water and nutrients at deeper soil levels, which is important during hot weather and droughts. During hot months, if you raise the cutting height by ¼ to ½ inch, the extra length will shade the base of the grass blade and help keep the soil surface cool and moist. Cut often enough to not have to clip more than one third of the grass length each time to keep the grass an appropriate length. Mow in different directions each time and overlap each pass by about four inches for a smooth, even cut.

The average lawn needs about one inch of water a week during the growing season and should be moist to a depth of six to eight inches. To help prevent diseases, water in the morning so that grass blades dry out by evening. If you water in the heat of the day, much is lost by evaporation. An underground sprinkler system can simplify this task and save water at the same time.

All lawns have some thatch—dead roots, stems, and grass clippings—on their surface. A thin layer of thatch will help a lawn retain moisture, and short clippings from mowings can help return nutrients to the soil. However, too much thatch can keep air, water, and fertilizer from reaching the grass roots. Since de-thatching is difficult and messy, discourage excess thatch buildup by following the guidelines given above for mowing, watering, and feeding the lawn.

If the soil is good and the grass is sound but sparse, a lawn can be rejuvenated relatively easily. Mow the grass to one inch. Slice or chop the lawn with a rake, hoe, spade, or cultivating tool, then spread fertilizer made especially for new grass over the entire lawn. Finally, spread the seed. Keep the surface constantly moist without causing puddles. If the soil dries out, new seedlings will die or new seed will not germinate. After four to six weeks, follow up with another feeding to help establish the new grass seedlings.

To seed bare spots in a lawn, start by loosening a half inch of soil with a spade, rake, or cultivating tool. Then lightly sprinkle the area with fertilizer and seed, and mulch lightly with peat moss to protect young plants. Be sure to keep the spots moist until the grass is well started.

STARTING A NEW LAWN

Before starting a new lawn or renovating an existing one, think about how much time, energy, and money you want to devote to it. Perhaps limited turf with a terrace next to the house and rough, less demanding grass or a wildflower meadow at the perimeter of your property would be more rewarding. However, for every lawn, whether big or small, the ingredients for success remain the same: good soil with adequate drainage, the right grass for your location and use, proper feeding, correct but not excessive mowing, and adequate watering.

A healthy lawn begins with the soil. If the soil is too sandy, it drains so fast that it washes away fertilizer before it gets to the roots; soil too heavy with clay drains slowly, retaining water for so long that neither fertilizer nor air can get to the roots. The cure for both conditions is to work a couple of inches of organic matter such as peat moss or leaf mulch into the soil.

Planting Sod

Planting sod instead of seed provides an instant lawn of healthy mature grass and eliminates the whole process of bringing seed to full maturity, which can take up to a year. However, sod is expensive, and in some areas the choice of turf grasses is limited, making it difficult to match existing seed if you need only to patch bare or damaged spots. If you do choose sod, it should be no more than one inch thick or it might be hard to establish. Check the edges to make sure the soil has not dried out. Also, look for grass that is uniformly green, with a well-developed root system and no weeds or brown patches.

To lay sod, first prepare the soil as you would for seed, but grade ½ to 1 inch lower to allow for the thickness of the sod. Lay the strips parallel, with ends staggered as in a running-bond brickpattern. Avoid stretching or overlapping. (Trim the edges of the strips if necessary.) Finally, roll lightly to ensure good contact between sod and soil.

Keep the lawn saturated during the first week, moist during the second. Failure to water is a major cause of sod-lawn deterioration. Begin mowing your new lawn after two or three weeks. Fertilize as recommended by the grower.

Light rolling ensures good contact between sod and soil.

The correct choice of grass seed is crucial. Since a single variety of a single species is too easy for insects and fungus to wipe out, use a mix, and one that is appropriate for your climate, soil, and exposure—sun or shade. Improvements are constantly being made in grass seed, so look for the new, named hybrids with shade, heat, drought, and disease resistance. Common components of lawn-seed mixes include Kentucky bluegrasses, fine and tall fescues, and turf-type perennial ryegrasses. The soft, fine-leaved bluegrasses are top choices for sunny yards. For plots that are dry and shady, the long-wearing fescues and fast-starting ryegrasses are practical. Make sure you know what you are getting. The extra pennies spent on named, high-quality seed, dated for the current year, are well worth it. The final lawn will look better for longer with less water and less care. Since your choice of grass seed will depend on the amount of sun your lawn gets, your particular soil, and the hardiness zone in which you live, let your local garden center, cooperative extension service, or other landscape professional help you decide what grass seed is right for your situation.

Lawns should be planted in late summer or early fall. Since new lawns need a good deal of water, do not seed in late spring or early summer, when dry spells are frequent. Follow these steps in planting your new lawn.

1. Measure your plot. Directions on packages of organic matter, lime, fertilizer, and seed are based on 1,000 square feet.

2. If your soil is poor, spread new topsoil evenly on the area to be seeded. Grade away from the house, patio, or pool area to provide for good drainage.

3. Mix in organic matter, such as peat moss, leaf mulch, or well-rotted manure, with a small rototiller or spade.

Before you do anything, test your soil to find out if it lacks any necessary nutrients or if it is too acid or too alkaline. Building healthy soil and grass roots is particularly vital if you want to avoid using chemical weed-killers, pesticides, and fertilizers to keep the lawn lush. Take multiple specimens of soil, to a depth of three inches, from different parts of your yard. Combine the samples, mix them well, and give a cupful or two to your cooperative extension service for analysis. Or, use a soil-test kit, available from a local garden center.

Grass grows best at a slightly acid pH level, from 6.0 to 7.0. If your soil tests less than 6, sprinkle the area to be seeded with limestone to reduce the acid content. (Lime also supplies magnesium and calcium, usually deficient in acid soil.) If the pH is above 7, the soil is too alkaline and may need sulphur. In this case, consult a soil lab or landscape professional.

4. If you brought in new topsoil, test it and add lime or fertilizers as needed. Till or rake these additives into the top four inches of soil as the final grade and planting bed.

5. Firm up the soil with a water roller to define humps and hollows in the new lawn.

6. Rake the surface lightly to level the irregularities and to prepare a loose planting bed of ¼ to ½ inch of soil.

7. Sow the grass seed with a drop-type spreader or by hand: Either will be uniform if the air is calm. For best results, divide the seed bed into several equal parts and set aside a portion of seed for each area. Spread half of the seed for each part in one direction and the other half at right angles to the first. Such overlap will avoid empty spaces in the lawn.

8. Rake in the seed lightly.

9. Firm the soil with a light roller or one with most of the water ballast removed, to promote seed germination. Then, to conserve moisture, protect the seeding with a covering of ¹⁄₁₆ to ⅛ inch of clean straw.

Water your new lawn frequently and lightly, using a sprinkler. Do not allow the seedbed to become dry or waterlogged. As the grass begins to grow, decrease the frequency of watering, but increase the amount of water each time. Normally, a two-month-old turf can be watered the same way as an established lawn. Start mowing as soon as clippings can be removed at a cutting height of 1½ to 2 inches. Then mow whenever the grass is one inch higher than cutting height. Keep your mower sharp or the young grass will be injured. Mowing should be the only traffic on the turf until new grass has filled in enough to hide the soil. Fertilize a fall-started lawn the following spring.

Since lawn care can be complex, and problems do arise, let the experts help. Local garden centers, cooperative extension services, and other landscape professionals are prepared to come to your rescue.

GROUND COVERS

Well-kept turf can be costly, and it requires a great deal of care. Also, in these days of recurring droughts and other ecological concerns, smaller lawns integrated with other ground covers have become increasingly popular. Not only are ground covers less demanding than grass, but they give your yard added interest, particularly when used in mass over a broad expanse. They tend to be informal, look natural, and usually need no mowing and little maintenance once established. These low-growing, quick-spreading plants are ideal problem solvers for many yards. A hard-to-mow slope will look far superior with a ground cover than with inadequately mowed grass; a walkway is more inviting when bordered with plants; a shady spot under a tree is easily rescued with a ground cover. These plants will even help control erosion and bind sandy soils. And, of course, their foliage and seasonal blooms provide textural contrast to the lawn and a change of mood.

The most popular ground covers include English ivy (*Hedera helix*), which tolerates sun and shade and will thrive from the northern reaches of Maine to the Southwest, pachysandra (*P. terminalis*), which is particularly effective in deep shade, and creeping myrtle (*Vinca minor*), which offers the bonus of periwinkle-blue flowers. But many others are available to meet different needs.

Such herbaceous ground covers as spring flowering lily-of-the-valley (*Convallaria majalis*), bugle (*Ajuga reptans*), and the large hosta family, die back in the winter but return each spring. Moss, ferns, and European wild ginger (*Asarum europaeum*) are happy in shade and moist soil. In sunny locations, creeping thymes (*T. serpyllum*) will form a dense mat between paving stones and sweet woodruff (*Galium odoratum*) tolerates partial shade. Heaths and heathers, which can flower for several weeks, will provide a colorful look along paths and entranceways. Crown vetch (*Coronilla varia*) will spread rapidly on steep banks, as will the fragrant honeysuckle (*Lonicera japonica*). Creeping juniper (*J. procumbens*), which grows in horizontal tiers, and cotoneaster (*C. dammeri*), which produces red berries that attract birds, are among the many prostrate evergreens that offer year-round color and need little care. This is only a sampling of the diverse range of plants, vines and prostrate shrubs that can serve as ground covers.

Ground Covers

NAME	ZONE/EXPOSURE/SOIL	DESCRIPTION	USE/REMARKS
Aegopodium podagraria Silveredge Goutweed	4/E,N/Tolerates poor, dry soil	White-edged leaves; unattractive white flowers in spring (cut off to prevent seeding)	Dark, shady areas; may be invasive
Ajuga reptans Carpet Bugle	3/E,N,S/Well-drained soil	Evergreen; shiny, dark-green leaves; bluish flowers in late spring and early summer	Substitute for lawn
Convallaria majalis Lily-of-the-Valley	4/E,N/Rich, acid soil with moisture, easy	Bright-green leaves; fragrant white flowers, followed by orange fruit	As border for paths or driveways; poisonous
Coronilla varia Crown Vetch	4/E,S,W/Tolerates dry soil	Small, bright-green leaves; pink flowers from summer to frost	Steep, sunny banks
Euonymus fortunei Winter Creeper	4/E,N,S/Needs part shade	Evergreen; dark-green leaves	Many varieties; can be trimmed in spring to contain growth
Galium odoratum Sweet Woodruff	5/E,N,S/Moist, acid soil	Lance-shaped leaves; white, yellow or maroon flowers in late spring	Rock gardens; small areas; beneath shrubs
Hedera helix English Ivy	6/E,N/Moist, rich soil	Evergreen; dark-green leaves	Slopes or flat areas; vine for wall or fence
Liriope spicata Creeping Lilyturf	5/E,N,S/Tolerates dry soil	Dark-green, grasslike leaves; purple-white flowers in summer	Substitute for lawn
Lonicera japonica Hall's Honeysuckle	5/E,S,W/Tolerates poor soil	Evergreen; deciduous in severe climates; dark-green leaves; white flowers late spring through summer	Slopes; large areas; vine for wall or fence; invasive; needs cutting back
Pachysandra terminalis Japanese Spurge	5/E,N/Well-drained, acid soil	Evergreen; light- to dark-green leaves; white flowers in early summer	Under trees; easy to divide for more plants
Phlox subulata Moss Pink/Creeping Phlox	4/S,W/Well-drained soil	Evergreen; small, olive-green leaves; white, blue, pink, red, or rose flowers in early spring and summer	Rock gardens; sunny slopes
Sedum kamtschaticum Stonecrop	4/E,S,W/Well-drained, sandy soil	Evergreen; tiny, light-green leaves; yellow flowers in late spring	Rock gardens; between stepping stones
Thymus praecox arcticus *(T. serpyllum)* Creeping Thyme/Mother of Thyme	4/S,W/Well-drained soil, tolerates drought and poor soil	Evergreen; tiny, dark-green leaves; white to pink flowers in midsummer	Substitute for lawn; between stepping stones; in rock garden
Vinca minor Periwinkle/Myrtle	5/E,N/Well-drained, slightly acid soil with moisture	Evergreen; small, dark-green leaves; blue, purple, or white flowers in spring and summer	Shady spots

TREES AND SHRUBS

Just visualize a piece of land stripped for a new development, and the contribution of trees and shrubs to the appeal of a house becomes obvious. Since such large-scale plantings make a dramatic change in the landscape, and because they represent a major investment, their selection is important in designing a property.

Shape is one of the most important considerations, especially in selecting trees. There are several basic tree shapes, although they are not always known everywhere by the same names.

One shape, fastigiate or columnar, has a narrow outline. Included in this group are such trees as poplars, red cedar, taxus yew, and arborvitae. These trees create tall screens and vertical highlights in the landscape. Trees can also be conical, or pyramidal, in shape. Most needle-leafed evergreens such as pines, spruce, hemlocks, firs, and false cypress fall into this group. They too are useful for screening and as windbreaks. Both the columnar and the pyramidal forms arrest the eye and add static points to the landscape. They also lend a neat, rather formal quality to the yard.

Another common shape is rounded and softly contoured. Spreading deciduous trees such as oaks, maples, birch, beech, and chestnut fit into this group. Dominating the landscape as lawn highlights, these trees are noteworthy for their specimen characteristics in addition to their welcome shade and colorful fall foliage. Their shape suggests more movement than the pyramidal and columnar forms.

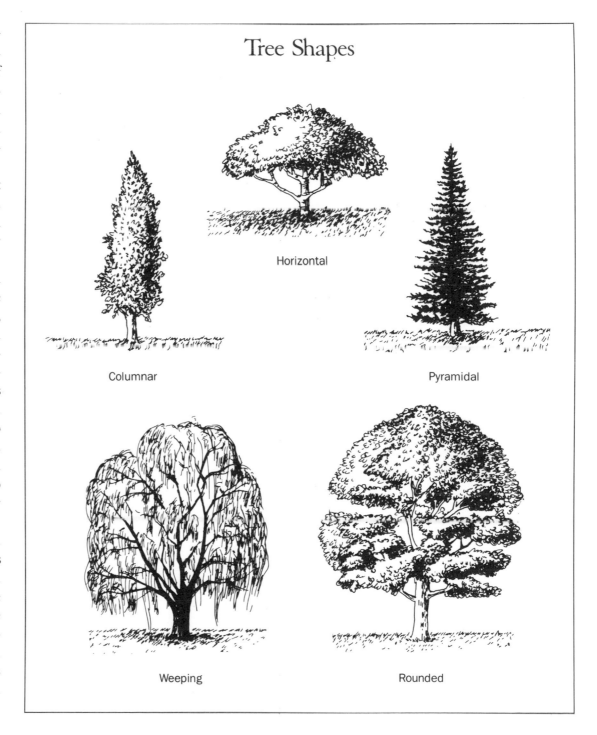

Tree Shapes

Columnar

Horizontal

Pyramidal

Weeping

Rounded

Planting a Tree

Trees are sold either in containers or with their roots balled and wrapped in burlap. Containerized plants should usually be planted in the spring. Burlapped plants can go into the ground any time up to 4 to 6 weeks before the first frost. Mail-order trees are often sent with bare roots. These must be planted as soon as possible after they are received.

1. Measure the diameter and depth of the tree's root ball. Dig a hole twice the diameter of the root ball and 1½ times the depth, reserving the removed soil. Work a few shovels of peat moss and a sprinkling of bonemeal or superphosphate into the bottom of the hole. Blend peat into the pile of reserved soil at a ratio of two parts soil to one part peat. Do *not* add any fertilizer.

2. Shovel enough of the soil/peat mixture into the hole so that, when you put the tree in, the top of the root ball is even with the surrounding soil surface. (To plant a bare-root tree level with the surrounding soil, build a mound of soil in the bottom of the hole.) Center the root ball in the hole and add more of the mixture until the hole is half filled. (Spread the roots of a bare-root tree over the mound and add soil as for a tree with a root ball.) Tamp down the mix around the root ball and water thoroughly. To eliminate air pockets, water as you proceed.

3. Cut the twine from burlapped plants and fold back the top. Remove any strings tied around the trunk and fill in the rest of the hole. Do not build the soil up the sides of the trunk. Using the extra soil, build a water trough around the perimeter of the planting hole to act as a reservoir. Flood the trough several times to ensure a deep soaking. Keep the soil moist, especially during the first year.

4. If the tree trunk is 2 inches or more in diameter, drive two or three wood stakes into the soil just beyond the root ball. (Stakes will ensure that the feeder roots are not torn away when the tree sways in the wind.) To fasten the tree to the stakes without damaging it, thread guy wire through short pieces of old garden hose placed around the trunk. After a couple of years, the root system will support the tree unaided and the stakes and wire can be removed.

Trees with horizontal branching offer still another look in the landscape. Some of these, such as the hawthorn, crape myrtle, Japanese crabapple, mimosa, and dogwood, are wider than they are tall, and some are taller than they are wide. The hornbeam, Southern magnolia, yellow poplar, and tulip tree fall into this latter category. There are also the weeping trees, such as the willow, Japanese or Kousa dogwood, weeping cherry, and weeping crab apple. These shapes add graceful, sculptural silhouettes to the landscape and are particularly effective against a skyline or reflected in the waters of a pond or pool.

Compact shapes used for hedges give a different outline. The dense, opaque growing habit of boxwood, holly, yew, and privet, for example, is ideal for screening purposes.

Although all members of a tree or shrub family do not fall precisely into one of these shape categories, keep the guidelines in mind as you plan.

In addition to shape, you also need to know how much space a tree will occupy in your yard when it has grown. A five-foot oak or maple sapling, for instance, can reach fifty feet or more in height and an equal width. If your space is limited, choose small- and medium-sized varieties instead.

What goes below the ground is also important in choosing a tree. The vast network of roots that anchors the tree and needs feeding can be shallow or deep. Shallow-rooted trees will absorb the nutrients of plants around them, but deep-rooted trees will not compete with surrounding plants for precious food and water.

Decide first whether you want your tree to be deciduous or evergreen. Although deciduous trees lose their leaves in the winter, bare branches have their own skeletal beauty and textural interest. In addition, during the summer deciduous trees provide cooling shade and can help reduce air-conditioning costs, while, conversely, in the winter they let in the sun to help heat a home. They are best planted on the south or west side of a house.

Evergreens retain their beauty and shape all year long and are a welcome sight on a bleak winter day. They can be broad-leafed, such as hollies, and rhododendrons and azaleas, or they can be needle-leafed, in which case they produce cones instead of flowers. Pines, spruces, firs, and hemlocks are popular conifers for decorative purposes as well as for privacy screens and windbreaks. Evergreens are favored as windbreaks, particularly when planted on the north side of a house.

Weeping trees can be either deciduous or evergreen, and should be considered for small gardens or for containers on a terrace. Among the easy-to-grow deciduous weepers are the Red Jade flowering crab apple, Japanese dogwood, Siberian pea, White Fountain cherry, and Youngii birch. Some evergreen choices include the Alaskan false cypress, American arborvitae, blue Atlas cedar, and Sargent hemlock.

Shrubs offer year-round pleasure in the yard and need the same thoughtful planning as trees. In some cases, the line between trees and shrubs is fuzzy, such as with the many small evergreens that are used as shrubs for foundation plantings, hedges, and privacy screens. The features that essentially distinguish shrubs from trees are their multiple trunks or stems and the fact that they remain relatively small when mature—at most about fifteen feet high. This woody nature also sets shrubs apart from herbaceous plants, such as perennials, which die back to the ground each year.

Often referred to as the workhorse of the garden, shrubs can be used as borders separating one part of the yard from an-

Transplanting a Tree

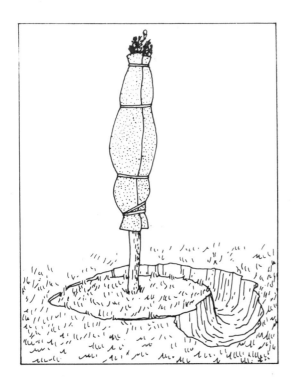

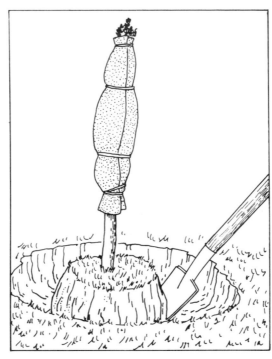

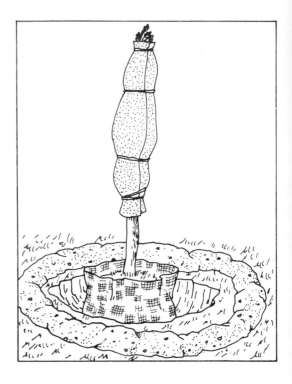

1. Carefully tie the branches of the tree together or wrap in burlap. Using a sharp spade, make vertical cuts in the soil all around the plant, following the spread of the branches. Following these cut marks, dig a circular trench 1 foot wide and 1 foot deep, and sever any roots in the trench. (If possible, do this a year or so before moving the plant to allow it to develop new roots closer to the trunk, and fill the hole with light soil. Then cut any new roots in the trench before moving.)

2. Free the soil ball with a spade at a 45-degree angle to retain as large a root mass as you can handle. Tilt the root ball onto burlap or a piece of plastic sheet, wrap it up to reduce soil and moisture loss, tie the burlap or plastic around the trunk. Transport the plant to its new home.

3. Dig a hole twice as wide and 1½ times as deep as the root ball, reserving the soil you remove. Add a generous helping of peat moss and a few handfuls of bonemeal to the hole. As with planting a new tree, put enough reserved soil back in the hole to keep the top of the root ball level with the surrounding grade. Place the tree in the hole, then replace and firm the remaining soil. Do not cover the trunk of the tree. Mound the soil around the perimeter of the hole to form a well and water thoroughly. Mulch with 3 or 4 inches of peat moss to help retain moisture. If necessary, support with stakes and guy wires, as with new trees.

other, as a backdrop for flower beds, as foundation plantings, as hedges, as privacy screens, as windbreaks, and as ornamental highlights in the yard. Flowering shrubs, for example, can be star performers all year long: Blossoms in the spring create glorious color; in the summer the green foliage provides a perfect backdrop for flowers; in the fall, foliage once again takes center stage, but this time in an array of vibrant hues; and in winter a shrub may have bright berries that enliven the barren winter landscape. For continuity of bloom, you can choose forsythia and winter jasmine for early spring shows; follow up with quince, lilac, and azalea; and end the summer with potentilla, hydrangea, rose of sharon, buddleia, and beauty bush.

Other shrub options are practically endless, depending on their purpose. Some coniferous trees, because they are low- and thick-growing, work like shrubs. Mugo pines, for example, are effective in borders, in raised beds, and in containers in city gardens. Arborvitae, junipers, and false cypress make ideal windbreaks and privacy screens on rooftop terraces. The eastern red cedar, really a juniper, is commonly grown as a tree hedge or background planting, and a creeping juniper makes an outstanding ground cover. To hide an ugly house foundation, you can intersperse the colors of viburnum, daphne, azalea, hydrangea, hypericum, and potentilla with junipers and other evergrens to create a naturalistic design complementary to your house.

Hedges are simply shrubs that have been planted close together to form an unbroken line. They can be clipped and formal, or unclipped and natural. Because of their foliage, privet and holly do well for a formal look, as do yews, boxwood, Canadian hemlocks, and arborvitae. For a more airy, natural effect in a country setting, con-sider Japanese barberry, Russian or autumn olives, spirea, and forsythia.

When you plant a hedge, the space between the individual plants should be somewhat less than the width of a mature plant. For a formal, sheared look, you can plant a little closer; for informal, unsheared plants, allow a little more space. When used as windbreaks, shrubs should be staggered in a zig-zag pattern.

In addition to these basic considerations, some fundamental dos and don'ts need to be considered before you start purchasing and planting trees and shrubs. Don't plant a tree too close to the house or to other trees. This is a mistake that many homeowners make. For foundation plantings, leave a space of three or four feet between shrubs and the house, and choose varieties that will not block your windows within a few years. When making your selections, picture how the tree or shrub will look throughout the year, not for just one season, and plan for continuity of interest. Equally important, choose the biggest and best specimens that your budget and space will allow. Look for healthy green foliage and thick, sturdy trunks or stems. Short, stout shrubs are better than tall spindly ones. Select plants that complement each other and your house, and plan for textural and tonal changes of pace. Groupings of two or more shrubs are usually more effective as an entrance accent than a single specimen. Do not plant in rigid rows, so the shrubs have room to spread, and plant in the proper location so that the trees and shrubs get the right amount of sun. Finally, do give both trees and shrubs proper care. During the first year after planting, they need special attention.

Do your homework. You can look up the growth habits and characteristics of trees and shrubs in mail-order catalogues

Professional Tree Care

Trees represent a major financial investment in your property. Moreover, they serve a number of important functions: privacy, shade, beauty, and a habitat for wildlife. You may want to enlist the help of an arboriculturist in the selection, planting, and care of trees. These professionals are certified in the science and care of shade and ornamental trees.

As with any other professional, there are certain things you should expect if you decide to use a commercial arboriculturist. These include:

A thorough evaluation of the health and safety of your tree or trees

A recommendation of work to be carried out

A written contract for this work, including a firm price quote

A description of how the work will be carried out

An explanation of any conditions of the work, such as the extent of clean-up, responsibility for any damage incurred by the work, and so on

An explanation and offer of nonchemical pest controls

Fees for continuing maintenance of your trees

Finally, ask for a list of references and a certificate of insurance.

and in books. You can also consult with local nurseries, garden centers, and your cooperative extension service to learn what is suitable for your area and property. After all, the investment is probably a large one, and the planting should be for posterity—that is, for your future and that of the environment.

Resources

The following list comprises sources of items for the yard, from bat houses to barbecues and playhouses to pool lighting, including plant and seed suppliers. Most will mail a catalogue on request.

GENERAL CATALOGUES

Brookstone Company
17 Riverside Street
Nashua, NH 03062
Garden tools, sundials, furniture, flags, swings, and Pawley's Island hammocks.

Clapper's
1125 Washington Street
West Newton, MA 02165
Classic American and English wood furniture, a wide variety of well-made handtools, waterproof planters, and outdoor lighting.

Denman and Company
1202 East Pine Street
Placentia, CA 92870
Gardening tools.

Front Gate
2800 Henkle Drive
Lebanon, OH 45036
Decorative ornaments, stone sculptures, outdoor furniture, grills, and pool supplies.

Gardener's Eden
10000 Covington Cross Drive
Las Vegas, NV 89134
Rustic furniture, trellises, arbors, planters, bat houses, and garden ornaments.

Gardener's Supply Company
128 Intervale Road
Burlington, VT 05401
Cold frames, composters, tillers, and irrigation systems.

Gardens Alive
5100 Schenley Place
Lawrenceburg, IN 47025
Organic fertilizers and pest controls.

Hammacher Schlemmer
147 East 57th Street
New York, NY 10022
Portable grills and deck furniture.

Hen-Feathers and Company
10 Balligomingo Road
Gulph Mills, PA 19428
Planters, pots, troughs, benches, birdbaths, sundials, garden tools, and figures in lead, terra-cotta, and verdigris.

The Kinsman Company
Old Firehouse
River Road
Point Pleasant, PA 18950
Plant supports, cold frames, compost bins, arbors, and arches.

Mellinger's Nursery
2310 West South Range Road
North Lima, OH 44452
Gardening supplies.

The Nature Company
P.O. Box 188
Florence, KY 41022
Stone birdbaths, birdfeeders, Soleri bells, sundials, and pool toys.

The Necessary Organics, Inc.
P.O. Box 305
New Castle, VA 24127
Organic fertilizers and pest controls.

The Plow and Hearth
P.O. Box 5000
Route 230 West
Madison, VA 22727
Green River garden tools, birdhouses, birdbaths, birdfeeders, and bat houses.

Renovator's Supply
Renovator's Old Mill
Millers Falls, MA 01349
Reproductions of Victorian hardware and accessories, including spigots, sundials, lights, birdhouses, and weather vanes.

Ringer
9959 Valley View Road
Eden Prairie, MN 55344
Natural fertilizers, pest controls, and gardening equipment.

Smith and Hawken
P.O. Box 6900
2 Arbor Lane
Florence, KY 41022
English and Japanese garden tools, irrigation and sprinkler systems, wood furniture in classic styles, and fiberglass and plastic planters.

Walpole Woodworkers
767 East Street
Walpole, MA 02081
Rustic cedar furniture, swings, picnic sets, cabanas and other small buildings, and a wide range of accessories from weather vanes to mailboxes.

Winterthur Catalogue
Winterthur Museum and Gardens
Route 52
Winterthur, DE 19735
A good variety of planters and some rare shrubs and trees from the Winterthur Gardens.

Wolfman-Gold & Good Company
117 Mercer Street
New York, NY 10012
Birdhouses.

ANTIQUES

Irreplaceable Artifacts
14 Second Avenue
New York, NY 10003
Authentic stone benches, friezes, and statuary, usually one-of-a-kind.

Lost City Arts
275 Lafayette Street
New York, NY 10012
Antique accessories: urns, columns, furniture, cast-iron fences, lamps, friezes, and weather vanes.

Urban Archaeology
285 Lafayette Street
New York, NY 10012
Antique statuary, furniture, ornaments in stone, iron, and terra-cotta, and wrought-iron fences and gates.

ARCHITECTURAL DETAILS AND ORNAMENTS

Anderson Design
P.O. Box 4057
Bellingham, WA 98227
Red cedar garden arches and trellises, fencing, lattice panels, and gates.

Andy Brinkley Studio
P.O. Box 10282
4904 Highway 127 South
Hickory, NC 28603
Garden sculptures and fountains of brass, copper, and bronze.

Ballard Designs
1670 DeForr Avenue N.W.
Atlanta, GA 30318
Pedestals, columns, sconces, and gargoyles.

Bodoh Quartz, Inc.
1222 Fourth Street
Key West, FL 33040
Garden ornaments made from recycled copper, brass, and iron.

Bow House, Inc.
P.O. Box 228FG1
Bolton, MA 01740
Pool and garden structures, including bridges.

Cape Cod Cupola
78 State Road, Route 6
North Dartmouth, MA 02747
Hundreds of traditional, handmade aluminum and copper weather vanes, as well as cupolas, wall eagles, mailbox signs, weather stations, and birdfeeders.

Carruth Studio, Inc.
1178 Farnsworth Road
211 Mechanic Street
Waterville, OH 43566
Cast-concrete and terra-cotta wall plaques, birdfeeders, birdbaths, statues, planters, and garden accessories.

Cassidy Brothers Forge, Inc.
U.S. Route 1
Rowley, MA 01969
Custom architectural ironwork.

Robert Compton Pottery
3600 Route 116
Bristol, VT 05443
Stoneware fountains.

Cumberland Woodcraft Co., Inc.
P.O. Drawer 609
Carlisle, PA 17013
Standard and custom corbels, capitals, gables, and architectural trim, and Victorian-style gazebos.

Florentine Craftsmen
46-24 28th Street
Long Island City, NY 11101
Garden ornaments and outdoor furniture.

Garden Concepts, Inc.
P.O. Box 241233
Memphis, TN 38124
Pavilions, arbors, pergolas, bridges, gates, and garden furniture.

Gateways
849 Hannah Branch Road
Burnsville, NC 28714
Garden sculptures and ornaments made of hand-cast stone.

The Gazebo and Porchworks
728 Ninth Avenue S.W.
Puyallup, WA 98371
Rose-arbor kits, porch swings, and gazebos.

Haas Woodworking Company
64 Clementina Street
San Francisco, CA 94105
Standard and custom wood trim, brackets, and columns.

Kenneth Lynch & Sons
P.O. Box 488
Wilton, CT 06897
Fountains, pools, statuary, planters, benches, finials, and sundials.

Moultrie Manufacturing Company
P.O. Box 2948
Moultrie, GA 31776
Standard and custom cast-aluminum columns, capitals, and bases.

The Painted Garden
304 Edge Hill Road
Glenside, PA 19038
Hand-crafted iron structures, including trellises, arbors, pergolas, and benches.

Robinson Iron
P.O. Box 1119
Alexander City, AL 35011
Cast-iron fountains, statuary, furniture, posts, and finials.

Sun Designs
P.O. Box 6
Oconomowoc, WI 53066
Gazebo plans.

Vintage Woodworks
P.O. Box R
Quinlan, TX 75474
Victorian and country gingerbread trim and Victorian-style gazebos.

Worthington Group, Ltd.
P.O. Box 53101
Suwanne, GA 30355
Pedestals, columns, and capitals.

BARBECUES AND GRILLS

Barbecues Galore
14040 East Firestone Boulevard
Santa Fe Springs, CA 90670
Built-in barbecues, smokers, chips, and accessories.

Big Green Egg
3414 Clairmont Road
Atlanta, GA 30319
Heavy-duty ceramic barbecues.

Brinkmann Corporation
4215 McEwan Road
Dallas, TX 75244
Smokers.

Brookstone Company
17 Riverside Street
Nashua, NH 03062
Barbecues and accessories.

Chef's Catalogue
3215 Commercial Avenue
Northbrook, IL 60062
Barbecues, grills, mesquite chips, and accessories.

Dynasty
7355 East Slauson Avenue
Commerce, CA 90040
High-end professional smoke broilers.

Lazzari Fuel Company
P.O. Box 34051
San Francisco, CA 94134
Mesquite, apple, cherry, olive, alder, and hickory chips and mesquite charcoal.

Lynx
6023-25 Bandini Boulevard
Commerce, CA 90040
Commercial-style high-end stainless steel gas grills.

The Ultimate Cooker
803 West Fairbanks Avenue
Winter Park, FL 32789
Barbecues, grills, and accessories.

BIRDHOUSES AND BIRDFEEDERS

Avian Aquatics, Inc.
6 Point Circle
Lewes, DE 19958
Birdbaths, drippers, and recirculating bird ponds.

Duncraft
102 Fisherville Road
Penacook, NH 03303
Birdbaths, birdhouses, birdfeeders and birdfeed; specialize in birdhouses designed specifically for purple martins.

Happy Bird Corporation
P.O. Box 86
Weston, MA 02193
Birdbaths and watering devices for birds and animals.

The Plow and Hearth
P.O. Box 5000
Route 230 West
Madison, VA 22727
Birdhouses, birdbaths, birdfeeders, and bat houses.

Wild Bird Supplies
4815 Oak Street
Crystal Lake, IL 60012
Birdhouses, birdfeeders, birdfeed, and books.

CHILDREN'S PLAY EQUIPMENT

CedarWorks of Maine
P.O. Box 990-GD
Rockport, ME 04856
Rot-resistant, splinter-free cedar playsets.

Childlife, Inc.
55 Whitney Street
Holliston, MA 01746
Modular wood jungle gyms, swings, slides, tree houses, playhouses, and sandboxes.

Walpole Woodworkers
767 East Street
Walpole, MA 02081
Jungle gyms, sandboxes, playhouses, and cedar furniture.

Wisconsin Wagon Company
507 Laurel Avenue
Janesville, WI 53545
Wooden children's toys, including wheelbarrows, sleds, and Janesville wagons.

Woodplay
P.O. Box 97995
Raleigh, NC 27624
Modular redwood jungle gyms, seesaws, tree houses, swings, and slides.

FURNITURE AND PLANTERS

Adirondack Designs
350 Cypress Street
Fort Bragg, CA 95437
Adirondack-style chairs and love seats.

Adirondack Store & Gallery
109 Saranac Avenue
Lake Placid, NY 12946
Adirondack-style chairs and rustic porch furniture.

Amish Outlet
RD 1 Box 102
New Wilmington, PA 16142
Bent-hickory and plain oak tables, single and double rockers and gliders.

Barlow Tyrie, Inc.
1263 Glen Avenue, Suite 230
Moorestown, NJ 08057
English teak furniture.

Cape Cod Comfys
114 North 36th Street
Seattle, WA 98103
Adirondack-style furniture, wood chaise longues, porch swings, and picnic tables.

Charleston Battery Bench, Inc.
191 King Street
Charleston, SC 29401
Cast-iron and cypress benches.

Country Casual
9085 Comprint Court
Gaithersburg, MD 20877
English tables, chairs, benches, swings, architectural trellises, market umbrellas, and teak planters.

FrenchWyres
P.O. Box 131655
Tyler, TX 75713
Wire garden furniture.

Giati Designs, Inc.
614 Santa Barbara Street
Santa Barbara, CA 93101
Teak furniture, outdoor French textiles, market umbrellas, and pavilions.

Gloster Furniture
P.O. Box 1067
South Boston, VA 24592
Teak furniture.

The Greenery
3237 Pierce Street
San Francisco, CA 94123
Carved redwood weathered-effect furniture: benches, chairs, lounges, and tables; also pottery.

Hangouts
P.O. Box 148
1328 Pearl Street
Boulder, CO 80306
Mayan-, Brazilian-, and American-style hand-woven hammocks and hanging chairs.

Kingsley-Bate, Ltd.
5587-B Guinea Road
Fairfax, VA 22032
Hand-carved teak furniture.

La Lune Collection
930 East Burleigh Street
Milwaukee, WI 53212
Bent-willow tables, and chaise longues and sofas with canvas cushions.

Lazy Hill Farm Designs
P.O. Box 235
Colerain, NC 27924
Hand-crafted garden accessories, including birdhouses.

Live Oak Railroad Company
111 East Howard Street
Live Oak, FL 32060
Victorian-style wood-slatted benches with cast ends.

Moultrie Manufacturing Company
P.O. Box 2948
Moultrie, GA 31776
Cast-aluminum reproductions of Victorian and antebellum Southern chairs, tables, settees, and planters (special finishes available).

Newport Garden Structures
767 East Main Road
Middletown, RI 02840
Teak and mahogany benches, tables, chairs, and porch swings.

Park Place
2251 Wisconsin Avenue NW
Washington, DC 20007
Mahogany, teak, and wicker furniture, planters, and accessories.

Santa Barbara Designs
P.O. Box 6884
Santa Barbara, CA 93160
Outdoor umbrellas.

Shaker Workshops
P.O. Box 8001
Ashburnham, MA 01430
Shaker-style rockers and chairs.

Sun Teak
3529 Edgewater Drive
Orlando, FL 32804
Teak furniture.

Tidewater Workshop
P.O. Box 456
Oceanville, NJ 08231
Classic-style Eastern white cedar benches.

Willsboro Wood Products
P.O. Box 509
Keeseville, NY 12944
Rustic log furniture.

Zona
97 Greene Street
New York, NY 10012
English teak furniture, Southwestern style furniture and accessories.

GREENHOUSES, GAZEBOS, SMALL BUILDINGS, FENCES, AND DECKS

Amdega & Machin Conservatories
3515 Lakeshore Drive
Saint Joseph, MI 49085
Custom-design conservatories.

Archadeck
2112 West Laburnum Avenue,
Suite 100
Richmond, VA 23227
Custom-design decks and sunrooms.

BowBends
P.O. Box 900
Bolton, MA 01740
Gazebos and garden structures of classic design.

Cropking, Inc.
5050 Greenwich Road
Seville, OH 44273
Greenhouses and supplies.

Dalton Pavilions
20 Commerce Drive
Telford, PA 18969
Pavilions and gazebos.

Four Seasons Greenhouses
2988 Merrick Road
Bellmore, NY 11710
Aluminum and wooden sunrooms, sunroom enclosures, and greenhouses with single, double, and triple glazing.

Gardensheds
651 Millcross Road
Lancaster, PA 17601
Hand-crafted wood potting sheds and storage buildings.

GardenStyles
10740 Lyndale Avenue South
Bloomington, MN 55420
Greenhouses.

The Gazebo and Porchworks
728 Ninth Avenue, S.W.
Puyallup, WA 98371
Arbors and porch swings.

Heritage Garden Houses
311 Seymour Street
Lansing, MI 48933
Garden houses, pool houses, and hot tubs, in various styles including Victorian and Japanese.

Janco Greenhouses and Glass Structures
9390 Davis Avenue
Laurel, MD 20723
Aluminum-frame greenhouses, solariums, and sunrooms.

Oak Leaf Conservatories of York
876 Davis Drive
Atlanta, GA 30327
Custom-design conservatories.

Renaissance Conservatories
P.O. Box 10604
Lancaster, PA 17605
Conservatories.

Sturdi-Built Manufacturing Company
11304 South West Boones Ferry Road
Portland, OR 97219
Redwood greenhouses.

Sun Designs
P.O. Box 6
Oconomowoc, WI 53066
Gazebos.

Texas Greenhouse Company
2524 White Settlement Road
Fort Worth, TX 76107
Prefabricated greenhouses.

Trellis Structures
P.O. Box 380-GD
Beverly, MA 01915
Trellises.

Vintage Woodworks
P.O. Box R
Quinlan, TX 75474
Reproduction.

Vixen Hill Gazebos
P.O. Box 389
Main Street
Elverson, PA 19520
Victorian-style gazebos.

Walpole Woodworkers
767 East Street
Walpole, MA 02081
Garden sheds, cabanas, boathouses, and stables; also swing sets, arbors, and furniture.

Wintergarden
5153 North Clark Street, Suite 228-H
Chicago, IL 60640
Greenhouses and conservatories.

Zytco First Choice Solariums
70 Gibson Drive, Unit 1
Markham, ON L3R 4C2
Canada
Solariums, solarium roof and wall shades, and pool enclosures, including retractable pool enclosures.

LIGHTING

Copper Craft Lighting
5100-1B Clayton Road, Suite 291
Concord, CA 94521
Copper landscape lights in several styles.

Doner Design, Inc.
2175 Beaver Valley Pike
New Providence, PA 17560
Hand-crafted copper outdoor lighting fixtures.

Genie House
P.O. Box 2478
139 Red Lion Road
Vincentown, NJ 08088
Hand-crafted brass and copper outdoor lighting fixtures.

Hammerworks
6 Fremont Street
Worcester, MA 01603
Colonial-style reproduction lighting fixtures and handmade wall-mounted electric lanterns.

Heritage Lanterns
70A Main Street
Yarmouth, ME 04096
Colonial-style pewter, copper, and brass lanterns.

Idaho Wood
P.O. Box 488
Sandpoint, ID 83864
Cedar wall and landscape lights.

Stone Manor Lighting
6219 Porterdale Road
Malibu, CA 90265
Hand-crafted copper and brass landscape lights.

The Washington Copper Works
49 South Street
Washington, CT 06793
Hand-crafted copper lanterns.

PAVING SYSTEMS

Interlock Paving Systems
802 West Pembroke Avenue
Hampton, VA 23669
Concrete paths and walkways.

Paver Systems
39 Landstreet Road
Orlando, FL 32824
Cement pathways.

PLANTS, SHRUBS, AND TREES

The Antique Rose Emporium
9300 Lueckemeyer Road
Brenham, TX 77833
Old-fashioned roses.

Arena Rose Company
P.O. Box 3096
Paso Robles, CA 93447
Antique roses.

Beaverlodge Nurseries
Box 127
Beaverlodge, Alberta T0H 0C0
Canada
Hardy ornamental trees, fruit trees, shrubs, and perennials (suitable for northern regions).

Bluestone Perennials, Inc.
7211 Middle Ridge Road
Madison, OH 44057
Shrubs and perennials.

Carlson's Gardens
P.O. Box 305
South Salem, NY 10590
Azaleas, mountain laurels, and rhododendrons.

Crownsville Nursery
1241 Generals Highway
Crownsville, MD 21032
Perennials and ornamental grasses.

Eco-Gardens
P.O. Box 1227
Decatur, GA 30031
Herbaceous plants grown from seeds collected in the mountains.

Herb Gathering, Inc.
5742 Kenwood Avenue
Kansas City, MO 64110
Herb and vegetable seeds and plants.

Jackson and Perkins Company
83-A Rose Lane
Medford, OR 97501
Roses and fruit trees.

John Scheepers, Inc.
23 Tulip Drive
Bantam, CT 06750
Daffodils, tulips, and other bulbs.

Klehm Nursery
4210 North Duncan Road
Champaign, IL 61821
Bearded irises, daylilies, hostas, and peonies.

Kurt Bluemel, Inc.
2740 Greene Lane
Baldwin, MD 21013
Ornamental grasses and rushes, bamboos, ferns, and perennials.

Logee's Greenhouses
141 North Street
Danielson, CT 06239
Geraniums, begonias, herbs, mosses, ferns, and perennials.

Milaeger's Gardens
4838 Douglas Avenue
Racine, WI 53402
Perennials, roses, and native prairie grasses.

Nor' East Miniature Roses, Inc.
P.O. Box 307
58 Hammond Road
Rowley, MA 01969
Miniature roses.

Oliver Nurseries, Inc.
1159 Bronson Road
Fairfield, CT 06430
Rock-garden plants, conifers, reeds, and general landscaping supplies.

Pickering Nurseries
670 Kingston Road
Pickering, ON L1V 1A6
Canada
Old-fashioned roses.

Swan Island Dahlias
P.O. Box 700
995 22nd Avenue N.W.
Canby, OR 97013
Dwarf and giant dahlias.

Transplant Nursery
1586 Parkertown Road
Livonia, GA 30553
Azaleas, rhododendrons, camellias, and ornamental trees.

Twombley Nursery, Inc.
1163 Barn Hill Road
Monroe, CT 06468
Dwarf and rare conifers, rock garden plants, and perennials.

Van Bourgondien Bros.
P.O. Box 1000
245 Farmingdale Road, Route 109
Babylon, NY 11702
Dutch bulbs.

Wayside Gardens
One Garden Lane
Hodges, SC 29695
Plants, bulbs, shrubs, and trees.

We-Du Nurseries
Route 5, Box 724
Marion, NC 28752
Nursery-grown native wildflowers and Japanese plants.

Weston Nurseries
P.O. Box 186
Route 135
Hopkington, MA 01748
Landscape-size trees, shrubs,perennials, flowers, and fruits.

White Flower Farm
P.O. Box 50
Route 63
Litchfield, CT 06759
Bulbs, perennials, and shrubs.

Woodland Nurseries
2151 Camilla Road
Mississauga, ON L5A 2K1
Canada
Alpine perennials, evergreens, ornamental trees, dogwoods, azaleas, rhododendrons, and magnolias.

SEEDS

W. Atlee Burpee & Company
300 Park Ave
Warminster, PA 18974
Vegetable and flower seeds, shrubs and fruit trees.

The Cook's Garden
P.O. Box 5010
Hodges, SC 29653
Gourmet varieties of vegetables and herbs.

Harris Seeds
P.O. Box 22960
60 Saginaw Drive
Rochester, NY 14692
Vegetable and flower seeds.

Johnny's Selected Seeds
Route 1, Box 2580
Foss Hill Road
Albion, ME 04910
Heirloom seeds and seeds for northern climates.

Pinetree Garden Seeds
Box 300
616 A Lewiston Road
New Gloucester, ME 04260
Heirloom and compact vegetable seeds.

Richter's Herbs
357 Highway 47
Goodwood, ON L0C 1A0
Canada
Herb seeds and plants, including rare varieties.

Seeds Blum
HC 33, Box 2057
Boise, ID 83706
Heirloom seeds.

Shepherd's Garden Seeds
30 Irene Street
Torrington, CT 06790
European vegetable seeds.

Southern Exposure Seed Exchange
P.O. Box 170
Earlysville, VA 22936
Seeds and garden supplies.

Thompson & Morgan
P.O. Box 1308
22 Farraday Avenue
Jackson, NJ 08527
Seeds for all common and rare flowering plants, including perennials, annuals, vegetables, and trees.

Vermont Wildflower Farm
P.O. Box 5
Route 7
Charlotte, VT 05445
Various wildflower species and wildflower mixes.

Western Native Seed
P.O. Box 1463
Salida, CO 81201
Trees, shrubs, western native plants, wild flowers, and native grasses.

SPRINKLERS AND IRRIGATION SYSTEMS

DripWorks
380 Maple Street
Willits, CA 95490
Drip irrigation systems.

The Gilmour Group
P.O. Box 838
Drum Avenue
Somerset, PA 15501
Sprinklers, pruning tools, hoses, and nozzles.

L. R. Nelson Corporation
1 Sprinkler Lane
Peoria, IL 61615
Sprinklers, timers, irrigation equipment, and nozzles.

Rainbird Sprinkler Manufacturing Co.
145 North Grand Avenue
Glendora, CA 91740
Consumer, golf, and agricultural sprinkler-system products, with design guidelines for installing systems.

The Scotts Company
Marysville, OH 43041
Spray wands, lawn products, and sprinklers.

True Temper
P.O. Box 8859
465 Railroad Avenue
Shiremanstown, PA 17011
Nozzles, sprinklers, connectors, adapters, and start-up sets.

The Urban Farmer Store
2833 Vincente Street
San Francisco, CA 94116
Drip and automatic irrigation systems.

WATER GARDENS

Lilypons Water Gardens
P.O. Box 10
6800 Lilypons Road
Buckeystown, MD 21717
Water lilies, water grasses, bog plants, ornamental fish, ponds, and pond supplies.

Slocum Water Gardens
1101 Cypress Gardens Boulevard
Winter Haven, FL 33884
Water gardens, books, and supplies.

Van Ness Water Gardens
2460 North Euclid Avenue
Upland, CA 91784
Water lilies, fountains, filters, and pond supplies.

Waterford Gardens
74 East Allendale Road
Saddle River, NJ 07458
Water garden accessories, ponds, lilies, bog plants, and ornamental fish.

Jean Spiro Breskend gratefully acknowledges all the homeowners whose enthusiasm and love for their houses and yards made writing this book such a joy. Special appreciation also goes to all the architects and landscape professionals whose creativity and expertise could be passed along to the readers of *Backyard Design*. Thanks are also expressed to the experts in their fields who answered endless hours of questions, to The Writers' Room, which provided a serene, supportive atmosphere in which to work, to my husband, whose good humor and own experience with outdoor projects were invaluable, and to Smallwood & Stewart, who gave me the opportunity to become so totally immersed in the fascinating process of yard design.

Karen Bussolini gives thanks to the homeowners who graciously opened their yards to me, pitched in to help, and made me feel welcome. Special thanks to Marggy Kerr, Robert Richenburg, Theo Alexander, Bill and Marilyn Norton, Diane Moore, Peter Woerner, and to Ellie Casey, who introduced me to gardening friends in Stonington and took wonderful care of me while I worked there. My thanks must go to the designers, who are the real stars of this book. Jan Johnsen, and Don Walsh were especially helpful, as were Dick Ryan and Jeanne Allen at Dansk International Designs, who provided me with beautifully designed and coordinated table settings. Thanks also to my husband, John Scofield, who kept everything together at home while I and our unborn son traveled like butterflies from one garden to the next.

The landscape architects and designers whose properties are reproduced in this book are:

Tom Gilmore
Landscape Designer
Gilmore Design Assoc.
Westport, CT

Peter Gisolfi
Peter Gisolfi Assoc. Architects
Hastings-on-Hudson, NY

Tom and Ragna Tischler Goddard
The Sundial Herb Garden
Higganum, CT

Frank Gravino
Architect
New Haven, CT

Peter Alexander
Landscape Architect
Site Design Assoc.
Greenwich, CT

Ben Benedict and Carl Pucci
BumpZoid
New York City

Ellen Ebersole
Landscape Designer
Guildford, CT

Glen Fries
Architect and Landscape Architect
Glen Fries Assoc.
New York City

Jan Johnsen
Landscape Design and Construction
Mt. Kisco, NY

L.A.D.A. Design
Simsbury, CT

Marggy Kerr & Robert Richenburg
East Hampton, NY

Randolph Marshall
Landscape Architect
Katonah, NY

Bonnie McLean
Landscape and Garden Design
Ashaway, RI

Jeff Mendoza
J. Mendoza Gardens, Inc.
New York City

Lisa Stamm
Landscape Gardener
Shelter Island, NY

Donald J. Walsh
Landscape Architect
New York City

Peter Woerner
Architect
New Haven, CT

Smallwood & Stewart owe thanks to the many people without whom this book would not have been possible: The many homeowners who graciously allowed us to photograph their yards and houses and who answered many questions, and the landscape architects and designers, who helped us photograph the properties they designed and who shared with us a great deal of information. Particular thanks are due to landscape architect Don Walsh, who answered innumerable questions with generosity, interest, and clarity, and Kathryn George, for her expert styling and advice.

Jacket: property designed by Peter Alexander, garden design by Katie Brown

Half title page: property designed by Peter Alexander; title page: L.A.D.A. Design; facing copyright page: Lisa Stamm

Back jacket photographs by Karen Bussolini; designers, clockwise from top left: Lisa Stamm, Randolph Marshall, Peter Alexander, and Don Walsh

Line drawings: Ed Lipinski
Illustrations for story openers: Willie Sunga